dirty poker
the poker underworld exposed

under cover publishing

RICHARD MARCUS

First published in 2006 by Undercover Publishing

Copyright © 2006 Richard Marcus

British Library Cataloguing-in-Publication Data
A catalogue record for this book is available from the British Library.

ISBN 0-9551697-0-4

This book is published by Richard Marcus
www.richardmarcusbooks.com
www.undercover-books.co.uk

Also by Richard Marcus
Great Casino Heist
Identity Theft Incorporated

Printed and bound in the UK.

For Yuss

In certain cases the author has changed the name of players and tournaments to protect persons and venues.

CONTENTS

ONLY IN HOLLYWOOD AND VEGAS

A performing artist who has newly taken up tournament poker at about the same time she took up a tournament poker-playing boyfriend has stunned the poker world by winning the Ladies Championship at a recent World Super Bowl of Poker. Sounds like a great movie script, right?

Wrong!

It happened. And it's bullshit.

This win was bought and paid for with a little help from her poker-playing boyfriend and Hollywood contacts. Why? Because it serves both Hollywood and Las Vegas on a silver platter. The fact that a celebrity won gets the tournament more exposure and loads of favorable publicity. It also puts the performing artist back on the radar screen for entertainment gigs she might otherwise never have a chance of landing.

What I'm saying is that a deal was made to distribute her winnings among the other players at her final table so that this win could happen and make everyone happy.

Yes, it was a conspiracy. And there are many others going on in the poker underworld.

Want another example? How about the Fox Sports Net

mega-poker tournament slated for July 12, 2006? It's the richest poker event ever and will be broadcast around the world and feature six famous players, each of whom will put up $10 million for the $60 million winner-take-all jackpot.

Come on, gimme a break! If this isn't a prearranged hype of mega-crap to boost Fox's ratings while showing off the players, what is? First of all, what poker player in his right mind would legitimately put up $10 million to win $60 million against true odds of five to one? There's no value in it. Pro players only take the action when they have the best of it. What's really happening here is more mega-collusion between Hollywood and Las Vegas, where the six poker players become bankable movie stars for their "roles." The network in turn reaps millions in advertising revenues and a huge boost in its ratings.

And we will have to suffer this again in 2007 when the jackpot shoots to $75 million.

And again in 2008 when it rockets to $100 million.

Just a matter of time until they make it a billion!

FOREWORD: WHY THIS BOOK?

The first thing I want to make clear is that this book has not been written to condemn the game of poker or to take the position that poker is inundated by nefarious gangs of cheaters and dishonest people. Poker, like just about everything else in our society, is based on money, and wherever you have an entity based on money, be it industry, war, sports or gambling games, you will have a fair share of dishonesty and corruption. Such faults are at the core of the human beast. Consequently, dirty poker has its place in every facet of the game. You will find it in your home games. You will find it on the Internet. You will find it at the final table of the World Series of Poker Championship.

In the now hundreds, maybe thousands of books written on what seems to have become Britain's favorite pastime, poker cheating gets very little shrift: a few pages here, a few pages there. Many authors have dismissed cheating at poker by saying it is usually carried out by monumentally inept people who most of the time can't even beat the game with their outlaw methods. That declaration is untrue. The truth is that scores of very competent cheating teams are out there, and if you play the game regularly, believe me, you've been taken by poker cheats.

My personal feeling is that since millions of British and millions more people around the world invest substantial amounts of time and money in poker, they have the right to know everything that goes on in the poker world—including the poker *underworld*. Therefore, I am going to disclose everything you need to know about cheating, both in brick and mortar cardrooms and online. I will tell you how it's done, who does it and why (it's not totally about money), and what you can do to protect yourself once you've unwittingly stumbled into a rigged game.

Take advantage of what you're about to read in these pages. If you do, I promise you will save a considerable amount of money while playing poker. You will also learn a lot about the game. You will be made privy to things you didn't know, while finding out that things you thought you knew are not so. You should be quite entertained by some cheating anecdotes I will pass along. Perhaps more than anything else, you will be stung by the surprising revelation of who today's dirty poker players really are. Many of them have become bona fide celebrities.

Finally, you will notice in this book that I often address the reader personally, as if I'm speaking to "you." In some passages the "you" I'm referring to is the honest poker player; in others it's the poker cheat. In most instances, my indiscriminate use of "you" is only to facilitate the writing of what I'm saying. I am never intentionally giving advice or encouragement to cheaters. On the other hand, it is my intention to do just that for "you" honest players.

INTRODUCTION

As you probably already know me as the "ultimate casino cheat" profiled on Challenge TV's recent series *The World's Greatest Gambling Scams*, you wouldn't be surprised that I've been a dirty poker player ever since I was old enough to hold cards and count chips. Before I reached that age, though, I learned a very valuable lesson from my grandfather. I'll never forget it.

I was nine years old and I was with grandpa at the movies watching *The Cincinnati Kid* with Steve McQueen. I'm sure that if you're reading this book, there's a very good chance you've seen it. Some of you veterans of poker may have had the pleasure of seeing it in the theater, as I've had. But I'm not mentioning this because I want to tell you how sexy Ann Margaret was or that the rebel McQueen was my first child-hood hero. I just want to bring the film's final scene back to life because in a way it shaped my own life, and had it not been shot I probably would have never written this book.

Remember that classic last hand, perhaps the greatest hand in the annals of poker anywhere? The one that was more amazing than any hand you've ever seen in a real poker room or on a TV poker tournament or even in front of your computer screen logged on to PartyPoker.com. The one that even surpassed those doozie hands you'll never forget from the home games you played in your basement while growing up.

Of course I'm talking about the 10 fatal cards Lady Fingers dealt to the Kid and his nemesis, Lancey Howard. The Kid had been in command of their grueling heads-up fight to the finish, which had been going nonstop for two days. The elder Lancey looked haggard and ready to crumble, and the Kid was about to deliver the knockout blow. When the fifth and last card was dealt to the Kid, he was looking better than ever. That because he received an ace, giving him a full house of aces over 10s, a monster, a virtual lock winning hand in five-card stud. After all, how hard is it to get that same hand in *seven*-card stud? I know most of you don't play that game either any more, but you still know exactly what I'm talking about.

Well, Lancey Howard wasn't so impressed. His fifth card staring up from the table was the nine of diamonds. His three other up cards were also diamonds and, as we were reminded by Lady Fingers' gravelly voice, in range of a "possible straight flush." After the Kid bet out his two pair of aces and 10s on board and got raised by Lancey, and then had the gall to raise again, to which Lancey coolly responded by re-raising, my grandfather turned to me and said without whispering, "Richard, there's a cheating scam in the works."

"What do you mean, grandpa?" I asked him wide-eyed but with a little less innocence than most of my nine-year-old peers had.

He pointed an accusing finger at the silver screen. "Lancey's got the jack of diamonds in the hole."

I looked again at the hand but the camera angle shifted back to Lancey's face as he puffed his cigar. Suddenly he didn't look so beat up any more. Then the camera panned the Kid's face. McQueen was sweating. First thing I thought on seeing those rivulets drip off his forehead was that the Kid understood what my grandfather was saying. I on the other hand wasn't yet the sultan of cheating I was destined to become.

But I did figure out, the next time Lancey's cards were in view, that my grandfather was alluding to the possibility of his having a straight flush.

"McQueen's got an ace in the hole, Richard. You can bet your sweet little arse on that."

As I processed it all, some petty guy two rows behind us had the audacity to tell my poor, little old grandfather to shut his mouth. I wanted to verbally accost the guy and throw my popcorn in his face, but I was too intrigued by what everyone else in the theater seemed to take for granted, or just didn't want to have verbalized.

"The dealer's in on it," grandpa continued. "Lady what-ever-her-name-is fixed the damn cards. She dealt McQueen a full house, all right, only so Lancey could bust him out with a straight flush."

I was now hungrier than ever for the action on the screen. If there were one person on the planet in whose words I had faith, it would be my grandfather. To this day, so many years after his passing, I still have never valued anyone's words the way I did his.

When the hand played out exactly as grandpa had predicted, the Kid and Lancey re-raising each other until the Kid was all-in and in debt, followed by the dramatic flipping over of Lancey's hole card to reveal the straight flush which beat the Kid's aces-full boat, I realized my life had changed forever and that I would always beware of the rampant dishonesty prevalent in poker, as it is in every facet of life pertaining to money.

Yes, I know I'm confusing you, but you are reading me correctly. I still *believe* to this day—and I am widely considered to be the greatest professional casino cheater of all time, which if one thing does not make me an idiot—that the famous final hand in *The Cincinnati Kid* was fixed and that Lady Fingers, Lancey Howard, and even Karl Malden, who was portrayed somewhat in the film as the Kid's confidant, were all involved in collusion to have Lancey wipe the floor with the Kid's ass and cut up his money as soon as he was out the door. As a matter of fact, I'm sure of it.

How could I be wrong? I mean, just take a look at the hand: aces-full losing to a straight flush in a five-card game with no wild cards! I will not bother you with meaningless odds calculations. I will only say simply, Come on, if you believe that hand was on the up and up, then you've probably been a victim a lot more than once to the flocks of cheaters that swarm poker in all its vicinities. And you're probably the prince or princess of their prey.

Chapter One

Who are Today's Poker Cheats?

You're waiting for me to say "everyone and his mother," right? Well, it's not so. But that doesn't mean there haven't been hustling mothers guilty of cheating at poker. Grandmothers too. Poker cheaters come from all dimensions of life. They come in all shapes and sizes, too. Often they're people you'd least likely suspect to be cheats. Often they're people even *I'd* least likely suspect as cheats. Believe me, that's saying a lot. I have come into contact with hundreds of people who have employed fraudulent techniques to win at gambling. I had thought I'd seen it all.

But in September 2003, I was thrown for a loop while reading an article on the sports page of my favorite newspaper. The headline read:

Russian gymnast busted in poker cheating scam.

Underneath was a color photo of the beautiful Russian gymnast, Vera Shimanskaya. I couldn't believe it! The diminutive dirty-blond, blue-eyed Russian knockout was a goddamn poker cheat! Not only was she an Olympic gymnast but she was also an Olympic gold-medal gymnast. That's right, Vera won a gold medal at the 2000 Sydney Games. Later, unfortunately, the gold medals didn't seem to satisfy her any more. Vera wanted gold chips instead.

According to the article, Vera and her "Eastern European" boyfriend had taken to the Western European road as a he-and-she poker-cheating team. They were not at all of the nickel-and-dime bust-out variety. When Vera was arrested at a Spanish casino near Valencia, authorities claimed she and her partner had scammed poker players at that casino for $10,000. In one night! And that was only at the casino where she finally got caught. In the ensuing investigation, it was determined that the stylish duo ran up similar ill-gotten gains at six other casinos in Spain before their tainted luck ran out.

Imagine this, I thought putting down that newspaper. A graceful Olympic gold-medalist tumbling off her podium, spinning all the way down to the pits of poker cheating. What was the world coming to?

And then I wondered how they did it. The initial shock of *who* did it wore off, so I asked myself how an athlete such as Vera could go from Olympic sport queen to Madame Ripoff in so short a period of time. Was the boyfriend the real gaff artist and Vera just the sexy distraction? They must have done something banal to distract everyone in the whole goddamn casino. Something not unlike having Vera, dressed in a skimpy leather skirt with her leg muscles pumped up by stiletto heels, bend over in front of the poker table to pick up the lipstick she "dropped" on the floor, while her comrade switched in a stacked deck. That would seem the most likely way it went down.

It wasn't the case. It turned out that Vera had been playing poker regularly in several of London's card clubs, though she had never been accused of cheating in one. But somewhere in her brief sojourn as a poker player, she learned how to mark cards. In doing so she would have had to put some time and concentration into it, and then a lot of practice. I am not saying that the dedication to training as a card-marker need be as stringent as what she'd given to gymnastics, though Vera would have had to perform similar nimble twirls with her fingers in order to bilk 10 grand from a table of poker players. The Spanish authorities refused to give details on the exact method she and her partner used, though journalists reported being told it was very advanced.

If Vera Shimanskaya could be implicated in a poker-cheating scam, could the same happen to virtually anyone? Well, I would not go that far out on a limb to say *anyone*, but it could happen to a lot more people than you think.

Take a look at me, for instance. Do you think that while growing up flipping baseball cards, at a time when all my peers entertained dreams of becoming major league ballplayers, I had aspirations of becoming a professional casino cheater? Hardly. In fact, I *never* had aspirations of becoming a professional casino cheater. It just happened within my natural evolution, and when it was happening I had no idea it was happening. It was just the result of the progression my life was taking. I started off as a gambler, blew off my bankroll, got stuck in Vegas without a place to sleep or food to eat, and after crawling out of the gutter and becoming a casino dealer, I evolved into a cheat.

Most poker cheaters take a similar bumpy route. They start off as honest though losing gamblers, then turn to cheating to either recover their losses or just to stay in action. Many of these ill at luck gamblers justify their actions, blaming other players for their misfortune and sometimes even wrongly believing that these opponents were cheating *them*. Thus a little revenge would be in order just to balance the deck.

Some losing players cross over the line from normal poker

deception to cheating because they assume other players are cheating, without having particular players under suspicion. They merely rationalize the conception that if "I know how to cheat, then everyone else knows how to cheat, therefore someone *must* be cheating."

Many different mindsets can induce people to experiment with cheating, though I would definitely say that a history of losing at gambling is a prerequisite for making a career of it. Every person I've worked with in my entire casino-cheating career had some part of his life marred by destructive gambling. Those few gamblers, poker players included, who have that rare talent of consistently beating the odds would have no reason to adopt cheating into their strategies. They're enjoying themselves too much by doing what they like while making honest money at it. In conclusion, the vast majority of today's poker cheaters are players who have not had success gambling legitimately and are on a mission to recover their losses the old fashion way: by cheating.

There are people, however, who cheat for reasons other than the recovery of gambling losses, though they clearly form the minority. Of these, most are adventurers and thrill-seekers. They are people who like to take risks beating the system and attain a tremendous high doing so. These are the kind of individuals who might be inclined to get involved in identity theft and credit fraud, or jump out of a plane with a faulty parachute. While sweeping in a big pot just won on the sly, they welcome the thought of casino security swooping down on them before they could stack their chips, though they believe it will never really happen.

Other people are motivated simply by their own egos to cheat. The vast majority in this category are college kids cheating poker games online. Most have never even been inside a real casino or cardroom. Instead of hitting their schoolbooks after classes, they invent computer programs to cheat the thousands of fish swimming within the expanding universe of online poker. Many say they cheat simply for kicks, but when you have kids still suffering from acne risking prison to hack into online sites, you can readily believe it's more about ego than anything else.

A final group of poker cheaters, the smallest, is made up of employees (or ex-employees) from the poker industry, mainly dealers and other personnel from live poker rooms who have grievances against the gambling establishments they work for. Unlike disgruntled postal employees known to go get their guns and rampage the facilities they work in, poker dealers take up cheating in collusion with players to exact compensation for whichever injustices they feel they suffered at the hands of their employers. In following chapters we will see how all these eclectic cheaters function and siphon off a sizeable share of money from the poker world.

Chapter Two

The Underworld of Legal Casino Poker

I was first introduced to organized poker cheating by, who else, professional poker players. Sure, I'd cheated at poker before, but that had been back in high school. When the other kids in the game weren't looking, I'd quickly stack a deck and deal some poor kid playing hooky a big hand and myself a bigger hand. Then a war of raises would begin where I'd clean him out. But that was kid stuff, and I left it behind once I graduated into the sophisticated world of professional casino cheating.

In the early 1990s, when I'd already been a casino cross-roader for 15 years, I was introduced by a mutual friend to a poker-playing couple who had fallen on hard luck. At the time, I needed people to work in my casino pastposting operation. The husband, whom everyone called "Preacher" (because he spoke like one), was the real poker player of the two. His wife, Carla, a tall and thin, striking brunette, was an average player who'd for many years been patiently listening to Preacher's dreams and promises of winning "the big one," which of course was the championship no-limit hold'em event at the World Series of Poker.

Well, by the time she made my acquaintance, Carla was running out of patience while Preacher was even faster running out of chips. They both agreed to take a hiatus from the poker world (where they were—and still are—very well known) and join up with me. It was through them that I would later receive a thorough indoctrination into the poker world.

I trained them to become cheaters at roulette and blackjack. We got along fine together, and before too long formed a successful casino team. We not only worked Las Vegas, Reno and Atlantic City but also toured the world wherever we could find ripe casinos for the taking.

One of our favorite destinations was the Caribbean, especially in wintertime. Our island of choice had quickly become Aruba, which proudly calls itself "The Friendly Little Island," despite the recent highly publicized disappearance there of an attractive coed from Alabama. Not only did we find great casinos to cheat at blackjack and roulette, we stumbled on some of the hottest poker action outside the United States.

The best of it was inside the Ocean Cabana casino, at the time a dumpy affair filled with cigarette smoke and oily rich Venezuelans seemingly itching to throw away chunks of their money. The men seated around its six full poker tables wore slick light suits with opened shirts, and matched their women in diamond rings and necklaces jewel for jewel. When Preacher and Carla saw how loose these bronzed jet-setters were playing, they asked if I'd mind too much if we took a break from our cheating activities so Preacher could jump into the $20–40 hold'em game and make a killing. Nodding my head to say go ahead, the furthest thing from my mind was that the Ocean Cabana's poker table number one would become our arena for that night's cheating.

A few hours later, Preacher was stuck $600. He got wiped not only because of bad luck but also as the game was super aggressive, pumped up by a rule unique to the island which allowed players to bet the full $40 on the flop. Most of the pots saw someone inclined to do just that.

Preacher got up and bitched the words all poker players say and hear so often: "I took one bad beat after another." He went on to explain the ones we'd missed: pocket aces cracked on the river, then pocket aces that turned to trips on fourth street only to lose to a happy Venezuelan's runner-runner straight on fifth street. When Preacher took a few more bad beats after the break, he crumpled his last few $100 bills and squeezed them into Carla's hands while I stood by and watched hopelessly. He said to her in a self-deprecating tone, "Maybe you can beat these geniuses."

Of course she couldn't. And by the time she'd stopped try-ing, they had blown two grand in their fruitless attempts to take big bites out of the bunch of healthy-looking bananas sit-ting around the table. Normally this wouldn't have pissed me off, but it just so happened that the two grand Preacher and Carla blew was a third of our operating bankroll for the trip. Now we were light, and one of the dangers about any casino operation, whether it's cheating, counting cards on the square, or whatever, is to be stuck in a situation bucking the odds with short money.

To make matters worse, we couldn't find any good roulette wheels to beat. The blackjack tables were packed with a sec-ond layer of people betting behind those in chairs. In frustra-tion I muttered, "If only we could cheat the poker game."

Preacher and Carla looked askance at each other.

"Maybe we can," she said, glancing at me and then shrug-ging at her husband whose brows comically arched.

Ten minutes later we were up in their hotel room.

"It works like this," Carla said to me as she laid a deck of cards face down on the coffee table. I couldn't help but admire her even more when I realized this beautiful woman had as much a larcenous heart as I. If Preacher was the legit poker player, she was the cheater, and before long I would learn that she was as skilled cheating poker games as I was cheating casino table games.

Collusion

The first of many truths Carla told me was that organized collusion among groups of players was the most prevalent form of public poker room cheating. That was because it was practically the only form of cheating that could be done without involving *physical* cheating of any kind. There was no marking of cards, no stealing or holding back of chips, none of the blatant forms of cheating that take place in home games where cheaters are generally not subject to intervention by gaming authorities and arrest leading to jail time. Furthermore, it is virtually impossible to prove that collusion among players is ever taking place. About the only action you can take when suspicious of other players colluding against you in a public poker room is to get up and leave. It's probably not even worth the bother to make complaints to floormen. They can't do much about it either.

Carla sat down and laid a stack of chips next to the cards. She slid two cards from the deck closer to her, leaving them face down. "These are the two cards you're dealt in a hold'em game," she began with cheater's precision. "You have to let us know what they are, *exactly* what they are, so we can use that information to our advantage."

Of course I didn't bother asking the stupid question, but before I made that conscious decision not to bother, Carla was already answering.

"You do it with the chips." She went into a detailed demonstration explaining how poker players usually protected their hole cards by covering them with chips, and how that universal trait could be exploited to cheat them.

At first I couldn't believe it. Here I was, probably one of the best casino cheats in the world at the time, and I was being tutored like a child in the art of divulging what your poker hand is to your partners. It had been years since anyone taught me *anything* about cheating at gambling. But I sat back and watched and listened. Carla had my undivided attention.

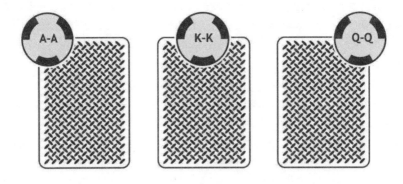

Note the chip placements remain the same no matter what position the cards lie on the table.

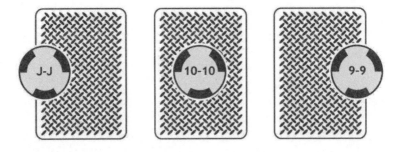

The way to communicate the value of your hand to your cohorts, as Carla explained, is to use your cards and your chips as a visual signalling device. Never use any form of communication that involves either your face or your body. To do so would be the cardinal sin of cheating at the poker table. I could relate to that well as my own casino-cheating operations were always carried out with communication in its subtlest form.

In Texas hold'em, the most important starting hands are high pairs. Carla told me that if I'm dealt a pair of aces, I must drop a single chip from my stack on the top left corner of my cards, which lie one perfectly atop the other on the table. The chip must be set half on and half off the cards so as to prevent confusion when reading it from any position at the table. One of the first things Carla explained was that you could never choose your seats at a poker table. You had to take whichever ones became available. Cheating at poker was not tailor made to suit your needs.

If my hypothetical good fortune allowed for a starting hand of kings, then I'd lay the single chip on top of the cards, but this time in the middle, again half of the chip parted from the card to lie on the table's felt. It was not difficult to guess where the chip had to be placed in the event I had pocket queens. I slid it to the top right corner as I watched Carla nod with a smile.

She showed me the rest of the signals for high pairs. Jacks, 10s and 9s followed suit by placing the chip from left to right across the middle of the card. So if I had a pair of 10s off the deal, the single chip would go dead center on the card. The chip representing 8-8, 7-7 and 6-6 would be positioned across the bottom of the cards, depending of course on which pair you held.

"Learn to place your chip quickly on your cards," Carla said. "You don't want to be out there looking like you're painting a goddamn logo on it."

I started liking this babe a lot more. They'd been with me a few months, and Carla had always been very functional and knew how to follow instructions. But seeing her now in a different light, as the leader of a cheating operation, was blowing my mind.

Of course I was a quicker than average learner. I imagined a grocery clerk would have a harder time getting on with this kind of signalling than an international casino cheater. In fact, before that first instructional session about poker collusion came to an end, I was already making suggestions as to how to improve *their* operation. One of them was constantly to play with and shuffle your chips. It seemed that nearly everybody did this while seated at poker tables, so an awkward silence at your spot would reverberate around the table, perhaps drawing other players' eyes toward your chips and cards to see *what* you were doing in lieu of incessantly twirling, spinning and mixing your chips. It was also best to remove your telling chip from the cards as soon as you knew your cohorts received the signal for their value. This could be done in a well-coordinated second.

Signalling became a bit complicated with high hands that were not pairs. There was A-K, A-Q, A-J and A-10 suited, and then the same hands offsuit. Then you had similar formations regarding lesser but still playable hands, such as K-Q and K-J, even Q-J and J-10.

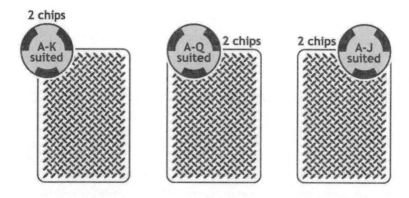

The first major difference in tipping off these hands to your partners was to use *two* chips. This made perfect sense because you had two cards with different values. With pairs there was only one value to contend with, so best was to use the single chip. When signalling high running cards such as A-K, A-Q, A-J or A-10, you used two chips on one of four different positions across the top of the hole cards. When your hand was K-Q, K-J or K-10, you used one of three positions across the middle of the cards. With Q-J or Q-10, you dropped to two positions at the bottom of the cards. J-10 was signalled by placing two chips off the bottom right corner of the hole cards. Hands with a top running card less than a jack were not deemed strong enough for signalling.

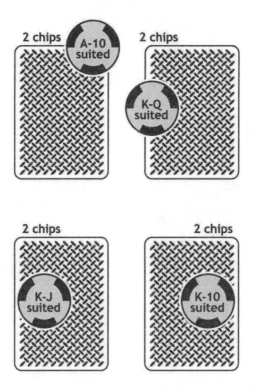

Carla took two chips and laid them on the top left corner of the card, exactly at the point where the single chip representing the pair of aces had been. "What do you think that represents?" she asked me with a smile somewhere between coy and seductive. I stole a glance at Preacher before answering, but he was already immune to her feline behavior.

"Gotta be ace-king," I shrugged. "But how do I know if it's suited or unsuited?" I thought I already had a pretty good guess at that one, but I waited for her answer.

"It *is* suited," she said, then quickly added, "I'd bet all the chips in this room that you could figure out why."

Preacher, who didn't speak much when he was annoyed or stuck money, decided to now. "There aren't many chips left in this room," he said rather glumly. "We left most of them in that idiotic poker game with those goddamn morons."

"Don't worry, honey," Carla said with a confidence I'd never before seen in her. "We'll get them all back."

I was quick to second her positive attitude.

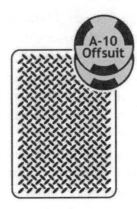

Carla turned back toward me while I studied the two chips on the card. They were placed precisely one atop the other on the top left corner. If you applied some kind of logical thought to it, you could tell yourself that something neat like that was "suited," thinking that it fit well. But if the top chip were tilted slightly off, you could, following the same logic, deduce that the cards in question were offsuit, thinking along the lines of being messy or out of whack.

When I verbalized my theory, Carla nodded her respectful affirmation then demonstrated how to cut the top chip off the bottom one to indicate high running offsuit cards. Preacher just insisted on knowing how much faster we could move along my lesson. At one point I had to remind him how patient *I* had been during *his* indoctrination into casino cheating. But to speed things up anyway and in response to my direct inquiry, Preacher said, "Don't worry about garbage hands. The signal is the same for all of them: no chips on the cards. The only thing you gotta know about unplayable hands is when to play them."

I figured that such a theory made a lot of sense in poker cheating.

The truth was, as Carla pointed out after 15 minutes of drilling on signals, that the key to cheating in poker by collaboration was the strategic use of those unplayable hands. Without them in the game you couldn't bleed out the money from your suckers. Excuse my using language like that to describe innocent victims of poker scams, but for now I'm writing this lesson as a cheater. Later, when I show you how to protect yourself from people like Preacher, Carla and me, I will address you in more polite terms, even though my use of derogatory nouns will probably have a positive effect on you. True, they will offend you, but they will also wise you up a bit.

The way it worked was that a collusion team's bad hands protected its good one (ones). Imagine a horse race with two horses coupled in an entry, one horse wearing number 1, the other number 1A. Usually the number 1A horse is only in the race to augment the number 1 horse's chances of winning the race, not to win it outright. For instance, if the number 1 horse were a good closer coming from behind to win races, the number 1A would be a speed horse trying to set a blistering pace to tire out the competition.

The same principle worked with professional poker cheaters on their green oval of operation. The bad hands have a specific function, which is to draw added money into the pot when a cohort hand is very strong. How do players holding weak hands do this? Simply by raising the bet when it is their turn to act and folding their cards at the right time so as to not create suspicion.

Carla painted a situation. Suppose, she explained, the three of us were working in collusion against a full table of $20–40 Texas hold'em players. Each of the players, including us, is assigned position numbers. These are not seat numbers, which remain stationary, but rather positions around the table that change after every deal in accordance with the rotation of the "button," the round disk identifying its holder as the player in the dealer's position.

We'll say that Carla occupied Position 1, the "small blind" where the player was forced to bet half the size of the lower limit for that game, $10.

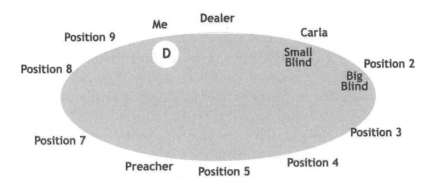

The person to her immediate left would be in Position 2, the "big blind," where you were forced to bet the full size of the lower limit for that game, $20. The use of blinds is what gets the action going. Then let's assume that Preacher was in Position 6, five spots to Carla's left, and I was sitting prettily in last position, on the button.

Being on the button is the most advantageous position in hold'em because it affords you the luxury of acting last. You get to see everyone's play before the action comes to you and thus you can act accordingly with that knowledge. Since poker is always dealt clockwise in conjunction with the order of the betting, you can always gauge the players between your cohorts to enhance your strategy. The cheating operation could thrive from any three seats, though it was best to be spaced out in order to have more leverage for the sandwich or "whipsaw" effect. It would also be less conspicuous than seeing players right on top of each other constantly raising and re-raising.

For argument's sake, let's say Preacher picked up a pair of aces on the deal, and Carla and I were dealt stiffs. The ensuing cheating scenario might play out like this: Carla is in the small blind, so her forced bet is already made. Position 2, the big blind, has also made his forced bet. The first player under the gun is Position 3, who calls. Next positions 4 and 5 fold and then it's up to Preacher in Position 6, who can play his aces either of two ways. He can raise immediately or have Carla raise when the action gets back to her. This decision is tricky and depends on many factors relating to the disposition of the game and its players. But for now, let's have Preacher raise the pot. Let's then assume that positions 7 and 8 fold, and Position 9 calls Preacher's raise.

Now the action comes to me sitting on the button. I have received Preacher's signal that he has pocket aces, by way of his sole chip having been placed on the top left corner of his cards. He has since removed that chip but I have processed the information.

I survey the entire table. Besides our cheating team, there are three players remaining in the pot, Positions 2, 3 and 9, though Position 2 has not yet been reached for action. I don't know if he's going to call Preacher's raise, fold his hand, or re-raise. Since a single raise in the first betting round of a full hold'em game is common enough, my best play is to not re-raise. At this point we only want positions 2 and 3 to call the single raise. If I try to get more money into the pot before the flop, we risk the chance of players folding and therefore the loss of forthcoming calls at the upper betting limit on the turn and river.

I throw in my chips to call Preacher's raise.

Carla, also privy to the value of Preacher's hand, has the same decision to ponder. Exactly what moves to make when you're working a poker table in collusion is based on theories virtually identical to legitimate poker. It's all about odds on your money and expected value. It just gets a bit more hairy because you're laying a lot more money against the pot, and if you lose, you lose three times as much.

Carla just calls, adding $10 to make her small blind a full bet and $20 to satisfy Preacher's raise. Positions 2 and 3 also call the raise, completing the first round of betting.

We have six players ready to see the flop, three opponents and three of us. If Preacher's aces hold up and win (or if by a stroke of luck Carla's or my hand wins), we need to suck out as much money from the table as we can. If one of the opposition draws out and beats us, we want to minimize our losses and regroup for the next cheating opportunity.

To keep the basic cheating strategy flowing, we'll have a flop of A♠-K♣-9♥. This makes Preacher's hand exceptionally strong. He's flopped a set (three of a kind) of aces, and unless two running suited cards come on the turn and river, there will be no flushes. There remains a possibility for an ace-high straight, but for the moment Preacher has the "nuts," meaning his hand is absolute best.

At this point we don't want to scare away the three opposing players. If Preacher raises when the action is on him, chances are we'll lose at least two of them. So what we want to do is maintain a balance of keeping players in the pot while reducing the chances of getting burned by one of them drawing out on us.

After the flop, the action begins with the first live player to the dealer's left, whether or not that position is one of the blinds. In this case it's Carla, who holds nothing in her hand, as I know since she never placed a chip on her cards.

Likewise I never laid a chip on mine, as my hand was 10♦-7♥. In the unlikely event one of us flopped a set, that player would briefly drop a single chip on the middle of his cards.

Carla bets $20 with the sole aim of building the pot. Position 2 calls but Position 3 folds. Now it's up to Preacher. Since we still have another player behind him, he just calls, and then Position 9 follows. I do the same. Now we're ready for the turn, the placement on board of the fourth community card where the real action begins—both the legitimate and the cheating action. On the turn you can bet the upper limit of the game (though in Aruba they let you do this on the flop).

The turn pairs the board with kings. The community cards now look like this: A♠-K♣-9♥-K♥. Preacher now has the monster: aces full of kings. I am now going to divulge that Position 2 holds A-K offsuit, which means his hand has turned into kings full of aces, another monster but second best to Preacher's aces-full.

Unless the river card is the last king in the deck, Preacher will win the hand. The odds of us getting burned are 43 to 1, provided that the fourth king had not been in either Carla's or my hand. Had it been, that information would have been broadcast among us, because once the board paired with kings we would have been alerted to the remote but dangerous possibility of Position 2's having quad-kings. In that case, we would have known there was no chance of Preacher's hand losing.

But even without the absolute certainty of being safe, those odds of 43 to 1 were good enough to raise the pot as many times as possible up to the "cap," the last allowable raise when more than two players are left in the pot.

With this information we can expect that Position 2 will invest a lot of money in his hand, in his assumption that it is indeed the winner. Our tactic is to drain as many chips out of him as possible, but at the same time remain careful not to tip off what we're doing. The one thing Carla and I cannot do is get into a showdown after multiple raises and then have to reveal the glaring impropriety of holding dogshit in our hands.

Carla can still come out betting as though she's trying to steal the pot. She does. Position 2 comes right out with a raise. Preacher "softplays" his hand and only calls the bet and raise. We don't want to tip off before the river that he's holding the huge hand.

Position 9 has seen enough and folds. Here, I have to fold, too. With Carla behind me, I know she can act as one side of the whipsaw while Preacher embodies the other. We can't sandwich Position 2 with three players, as that would be the worst "tell" of what we were doing. In some huge-pot situations, multiple hands can be used to manipulate the betting, but as a rule of thumb cheaters like to keep it limited to two, and vary those two players as much as possible. We don't want to show the same two players raising and re-raising each other too often.

Carla calls Position 2's raise, and next comes the river card. It's a blank (no help to anyone) but the hands are already made, two monster full houses.

Carla bets $40. She does this with the expectation that Position 2 will raise, and she knows that Preacher will re-raise. Her bet ensures an additional $40 deposit of Position 2's money into the pot since he would have bet had she checked.

Position 2 does raise Carla and is immediately re-raised by Preacher. At that juncture Carla must chuck her hand into the muck because she can't risk being exposed with nothing in a showdown. Besides, her mission is accomplished. She played an integral role in sucking out as much money from Position 2 as possible. By folding she has also nullified the cap rule.

Now with the action heads-up between Preacher and Position 2, unlimited raises are permitted until showdown. A victim heads-up at showdown is really hung out to dry.

Not surprisingly, Position 2 re-raises, exactly as we'd wanted. Preacher comes back over the top and the war of raises breaks out. When it's over, the showdown takes place and the cards are revealed. Preacher's big pair of aces out-shines Position 2's A-K and takes the money.

Of course this hand in the hotel room was all in theory. There are masses of variations on how cheating strategies adapt to the infinite situations arising in poker hands. My purpose here was to show you, with a high degree of accuracy, the way in which typical cheating scenarios based on player collusion go down. The intricate reasoning and mechanics of collusion must remain steady for it to be successful.

In seven-card stud, the signalling of colluders' hands is also carried out with the chip-card configuration, although it becomes more complicated because you're dealing with three starting cards instead of two. Most collusion teams will signal the value of the complete three-card starting hands, including those that have both running straight and flush potential. The signals are basically the same as I've shown for hold'em. Whereas in hold'em two neatly stacked chips on the top left corner of the card depict A-K suited, in stud it would mean A-K-Q suited. The same two chips on the top middle of the card would signify A-K-J suited. Two uneven chips in the same locations represent the same hands *offsuit*.

Starting pairs are signalled the same way as in hold'em, with the use of a single chip. Very advanced teams will even signal the kicker card to go with the pair, either simultaneously or by use of a second signal. Communicating starting trips is relatively easy. Preacher and Carla signalled rolled-up trips by placing three chips on the center of the hole cards. It was not necessary to signal what the value of the trips was since the two cards in the hole obviously matched the door-card (up card).

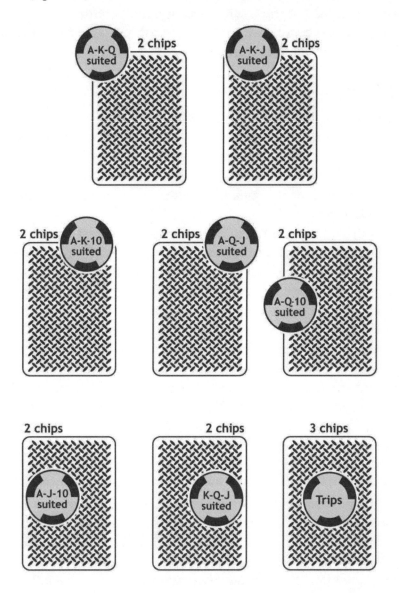

Some teams only signal hole cards and have their members mentally add the door-cards to it, totalling the hands. Personally I find that system to be cumbersome, but perhaps teams using it feel that three-card-starting hands are too difficult to deal with, especially when dealing with pairs and kickers or three-card straights and flushes.

The real thing

Now let's move on to live collusion. After two hours of Carla's tutelage, and thanks to my God-given abilities to grasp any cheating situation to which I had previously been foreign, we were ready to go back down to the casino and take our crack at the wealthy Venezuelans gathered around the poker table.

By the time the three of us got seats in the fast-action $20–40 hold'em game, the complexion of it had dramatically changed. There was still a load of high-rolling Venezuelans, but their dominance on the table had been weakened by the presence of an interesting trio of characters. Before the button made its first tour around the table, I learned who these people were. One was a guy I will call Rick Sayers, who was quite the redoubtable character of Aruban casino lore.

An American who had been formally charged with murder back home and was currently free on bail, Sayers had somehow penetrated the Italian (from Italy not the US) Mafia's stronghold on Aruban casinos. He was the owner of the very casino we were playing in, and had I known all this while seated at that table, I most probably would have signalled Carla and Preacher not what I held in my hand but only that I wanted to get my ass the hell out of there "as quick as I can!"

I had always known that the island of Aruba was game for loads of illicit stuff, especially in the casinos. It was a place that reeked of "every which way you can," especially for employees robbing casinos they worked in. In the mid-1980s while working Aruba with my pastposting team, we were approached by a few dealers in one of the casinos wanting to recruit us in their brazen embezzlement scam against their employer. Apparently they knew who we were from our previous visits there. We agreed to participate, and they dumped thousands of dollars in chips to us. It was quick and clean, and they managed to keep their casino bosses in the dark.

Another time on the island, I was cashing out chips at the casino cage and received a curious bonus. I laid down 20 black chips, $2,000, and the cashier paid me 40 $100 bills, $4,000. That time I was not in cahoots with any casino personnel, and no way did that cashier make an honest mistake. I concluded that he probably mistook me for the bagman in another dumping operation against the casino. So when I found out that Rick Sayers was an accused murderer moonlighting as a poker player, I was not at all surprised.

Sayers was also very well known in Las Vegas, as he was in Carson City at the Nevada Gaming Control Board's offices. With the arrival of the new-table-games-development craze in the early 1990s, during which we were introduced to Caribbean Stud, Let it Ride and Pai Gow Poker, among others, a big scandal broke loose and spread through the poker world. Sure enough, Rick Sayers was right in the middle of it.

It concerned one of these new games that hit Nevada's casinos, which I will call "Tropical Poker." This simple derivative of draw poker that was "casinoized" in 1992 took the casino world by storm the way online poker did the poker world a decade later. According to poker room gossip, which I can state with a high degree of confidence is accurate, the game was actually invented, or at least the concept was, by a down and out poker player who was more out as a result of alcohol consumption than down because of bad beats at the tables.

After having stumbled onto his idea for Tropical Poker, he took it to a high-profile poker player who today is world famous as an author of poker strategy books. This guy, whose name I will not mention but which most of you probably already guessed, did the math on the bust-out's game and concluded Tropical Poker was a viable new table game to introduce to the casino industry.

At the time, the Las Vegas strip was desperate for something of the likes to offset its clients' propensity of moving more and more to slot machines in the abandonment of table games. Casinos surely did not suffer from the waves of slot-mania pouring over Nevada and New Jersey, although bosses did not want to see their once haloed rows of blackjack and craps pits washed completely away by more of them. The time was perfect for the introduction of catchy new table games.

Happy as ever to hear that his game, in the opinion of the poker author, had enormous sales potential, the bust-out gladly entered into a 50–50 agreement to market the new game together. Only problem was that before they got their deal in writing, the bust-out ran off to Aruba with what little cash he had to celebrate, and met up with a hot Aruban barmaid who got him to hang around the island just long enough to get her pregnant.

Soon the bust-out, who at this point in the story deserves a name (Arnold), met Rick Sayers at the Ocean Cabana's poker game. While gulping the third or fourth of many beers, he told Sayers all about Tropical Poker. He even showed him the author's calculations proving the game yielded an ideal drop for the casinos. Sayers, being the Machiavellian entrepreneur he was, wasted no time in patting Arnold on the back, telling him how great his idea was, and then stealing it.

The next day, Sayers commissioned his carpenters to build an experimental Tropical Poker table, which he had placed in the center of his casino. The Venezuelans began playing it, and they loved it. It caught on like fire with the South American set. But it still took more than a year before Sayers brought it to the Nevada Gaming Control Board as an application for a new table game. The holdup was that Sayers, still mired in serious US legal problems, would never pass muster with the Control Board's background check.

I would learn of this difficulty firsthand, because back in 1995 I submitted my own new game to the Nevada Gaming Control Board (NGCB), whose chairman didn't want Richard Marcus involved in the state's casinos in any way. But since I had never been charged with a crime in Nevada, the Board had no choice but to grant me permission to put my game, called Action Odds Baccarat, up for field trial in Harrah's Las Vegas in June 1995. Unfortunately, the Asians I had counted on for action did not show any interest in leaving their customary baccarat tables to play at mine.

Sayers, in his case, needed someone to front his application to the NGCB, and by the time he found that person both Arnold and his author-partner were dealt right out. When the NGCB reluctantly approved Tropical Poker to be marketed to Nevada's casinos, Sayers made a fortune. He struck a deal with each Nevada casino to pay a monthly rental for each Tropical Poker table on its floor. Then he went partners with a Nevada gaming technology company to build a progressive jackpot feature into the game. Soon the strip casinos in Las Vegas each had a dozen or more tables, and with its huge cash jackpots the game's popularity spread like wildfire, burning swathes of casino space through Atlantic City, Puerto Rico and, before too long, the entire gambling world.

But poor Arnold and the poorer author got nothing for

their involvement. The reason for my using the demonstrative
form of the adjective for the author is because Arnold eventually managed to get something out of his creative idea. Although I cannot verify what Arnold told me when I went to
him for advice on marketing Action Odds Baccarat, he
claimed that Rick Sayers had agreed to give him $5,000 in
cash each month for 10 years. It was a kind of under-the-table
finder's fee to keep Arnold happy and his mouth shut. I later
assumed this to be true because at the beginning of each subsequent month, Arnold had pockets full of cash, only to lose it
playing poker and stay broke until the first day of the following month when he was pumped again.

The second character arousing curiosity at that poker table
was a guy who called himself Swat because his Arabic name,
according to him, was too difficult to pronounce, even for the
native Arubans who all spoke four languages. Swat was the
manager of the Americana casino down the road and, if you
believed him, also owned some points in it. He was a
swashbuckling Lebanese who had three beautiful women
fighting for his two arms while he gambled. He played poker
with reckless abandon, emitting the constant chatter of a
Turkish bazaar hawker. It was at his behest that the game, in
midstride, suddenly jumped to $40–80, which in view of our
diminished bankroll made our allowable margin for error
much thinner. In short, we had to do some good cheating
right away.

The third non-Venezuelan at the table was a transplanted
New Yorker who for some reason was being called "Tex." He
did, however, look the role with his Stetson hat and big belly,
but when he said even one-syllable words like "check" and
"raise" there was no hiding his origins. He'd been living on
the island for 10 years and was clearly well ingratiated with
the two casino heads.

As the cards for our first hand began flying, I thought that this trio would be formidable opposition not easily turned into victims. However, if we cheated our cards right we'd do okay. Our seats around the table were spread out enough to maximize the whipsaw effect. The last scenario you wanted was the members of your crew sitting next to one another. In that fashion, your raising and re-raising would stick out like a bulge forming at one end of the table.

But presently Carla was in Seat 1, to the immediate left of the dealer, while Preacher was in Seat 4, three spots clockwise from Carla. I was in Seat 7, sandwiched between Sayers on my right and Swat on my left.

None of us played the first half-dozen hands. We had decided in the elevator coming down that we would only play high pairs, any A-K, as well as A-Q, A-J and A-10 suited. In situations where one of us had a playable hand, we would alternate the other two players' entrance into the pot. Even though it was to our advantage to have all three of us in as many pots as possible, we had to mix things up a bit so as to not give the impression we played poker like triplets wearing identical dresses.

We had briefly discussed some of the subtleties involved in this kind of operation, and the tiniest of camouflage measures was at the top of that list. Other subtleties included never picking your cards up after the initial glance, as that could draw unnecessary attention to your hand and chips, and never trying to hide the fact you were winning money. Lots of players with mushrooming stacks of chips can be heard lamenting how many times they've bought in or other false statements lending credence to losing poker sessions.

Our first collusion in real poker took place on the seventh hand of the evening. Our actual seats around the table were the same but our positions for the hand had rotated.

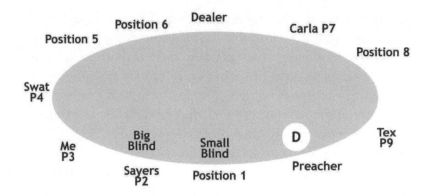

I was now in Position 3, under the gun because I was first to act after the forced small and big blinds. Carla occupied Position 7, and Preacher was in mighty Position 10, the button. He held the strong hand of A♥-Q♥. Hands like that on the button could really be referred to as sitting pretty. He signalled us his A-Q suited by laying two perfectly aligned chips on the top middle portion of his cards. My hand was a pair of 5s, not all that bad itself, and Carla had blanks (nothing).

I led off betting $40, laying a green $25 chip and three red $5 chips in front of my cards. Swat in Position 4 folded. Position 5 called. Position 6 folded. Carla in Position 7 called. Next Position 8 raised, prompting Tex in Position 9 to fold. Preacher on the button called my bet and Position 8's raise, while the small blind folded. Sayers in the big blind called. Then I called Position 8's raise, as did Position 5 and Carla. Finally the dealer swept all the chips to the middle of the table, forming the pot.

The flop came J♦-10♥-4♥. This was very hospitable for Preacher's hand, giving him the nut flush draw in hearts. But he still needed to draw out to win. Neither Carla's hand nor mine improved, but at this point our presence in the pot was more important than the value of our cards. Our function no longer consisted of winning the hand. Instead it was to protect Preacher's while creating the largest pot possible, once we determined his hand was the favorite to win at showdown.

But many things had to go right on the turn and river for this victory to materialize.

Sayers was the first to act in Position 2, which had been the big blind. He checked to me. I checked to Position 5, who did the same. Carla checked as well. The table was playing cautiously and waiting to see what Position 8, the raiser before the flop, would do after seeing the three community cards in the middle of the table.

Position 8 bet $40, and everyone called. The dealer turned the fourth community card. Bingo! It was the 7♥, giving Preacher his nut flush. The cards in the middle now looked like this: J♦-10♥-4♥-7♥.

Based on Position 8's raise before the flop and his lead bet after it, we put him on a high pocket pair that might have now turned into trips. He could have very well been dealt J-J or 10-10, which meant he had a very strong hand but could not win the pot unless the board paired, giving him a full house.

Sayers, again the first to act, grunted and tossed his cards into the muck. He'd probably had a straight draw, but didn't bother chasing it once he saw that his possible straight could succumb to a flush. I decided to check, looking to stay in the appearance of legitimate play. Position 5 checked as well. But Carla bet $80, the upper limit bet dictated by the turn.

Her move was strategic because now Position 8 was sandwiched between Carla and Preacher and would be ripe for a brutal whipsawing. We were hoping he had trips and could be bullied into paying a bundle to see the river card. There'd be no way he'd raise, unless he was just a foolish player. The three hearts were out there on board, and even if he had two more in the pocket—which was unlikely—he would know his flush could be beaten by a higher flush.

Position 8 simply called, thus we knew that if the board paired on the river we'd be in trouble. But Preacher had to raise in spite of that worry. We had much the best of it and therefore had to make Position 8 pay to draw out. If we got burned we got burned; that was the nature of the beast. In the long run the odds were with us. Only problem was that since we were on short bankroll in a game whose stakes threatened us with ruin, we had to win fast.

After Preacher's raise, I folded. Position 5 folded, and then Carla threw in an additional $80 to call. Carla would no doubt be tossing her cards into the muck after the dealer turned the river card. Again, she could not afford to be trapped in a showdown with cards that did not warrant going the distance. Another thing Carla had mentioned upstairs that worried me was that sometimes, albeit on rare occasion, a suspicious player winning a pot you folded on demanded that your cards be removed from the muck and shown to the table. If you were exposed in such fashion, there would be no doubt you were working a scam to jack up the pots for your partners. The only way to avoid blowing your cover like that was to expertly hide your acts of collusion. There was a delicate trade-off between shrewd play and avoiding detection.

Now heading to the river, the Venezuelan in Position 8 was sandwiched between Carla and Preacher, who had the top hand. That's exactly how collusion players want their victim. With such positioning they can hit him back and forth like a Ping-Pong ball. Fortunately for us, the card on fifth street was a blank, preserving Preacher's nut flush.

Carla, the first live hand to the left of the button, led off the action by checking. She could no longer bet knowing she would fold on Preacher's upcoming raise. As expected,

Position 8 checked, then Preacher made his $80 bet. Carla folded, and the Venezuelan who had fallen prey to our collusion called. Preacher flipped over his cards to reveal the flush. Position 8 gave that typical frustrated nod of "callers" at showdown with second best hand. He showed his pocket 9s and tossed them in the muck. The dealer pushed heaps of chips toward Preacher, who tossed her a $5 chip in return.

Our first hand in collusion was a winner.

After three hours of playing in that freewheeling $40–80 hold'em game, we had it beat for five grand. I fell right into the groove with Carla's and Preacher's signals and marvelled at how easy it was. Somewhere during that experience, I told myself that there must be hordes of poker cheaters crisscrossing the globe in pursuit of similar operations. Even at the time, poker was already huge, albeit not quite like it is today with TV coverage and Internet play, but certainly widespread enough to attract bands of cheaters chasing all that loose money.

During our play, a few phenomenal situations had developed. In one large and incredible pot, Carla and Preacher both had a pair of kings on the deal. I had a strong A-Q suited.

In the betting round before the flop, Carla just called the big blind from Position 3, and Tex raised her from Position 5. Preacher called as well from Position 6, despite the fact we knew his and Carla's hands were identical—and dead in the water as far as drawing trips was concerned. But, on the other hand, they would be able to whipsaw all the way to showdown, if it became necessary to unleash a series of raises on the turn and river. Losing bang-bang pots with pocket kings did not frequently generate suspicion.

Sayers and two of the Venezuelans also called Tex's raise. The pot already looked pretty healthy and gave the impression it might end up forming a mountain.

After a flop of A♦-A♣-8♣, with a club flush possibility, my hand replaced Carla's and Preacher's as our strongest. Carla bet $40 and Tex only called, but one of the Venezuelans in late position raised $40. Preacher called, and after a moment's reflection I called without re-raising. Then Tex pulled a sneaky check-raise and upped it the $80 permissible by Aruban rules. We really had no gauge on what his hand contained, but there was no way we could abandon the pot when I was sitting there with trip-aces and top kicker (queen).

Then a deuce came on the turn and forestalled the flush possibilities, while completely knocking out any chance of a straight. Carla checked to Tex, who bet out. I called, and the Venezuelan followed. Preacher and Carla chucked their hands. The river card was a 3 and knocked out the latent flushes. Then when I bet out, Tex raised me, giving sudden rise to the possibility he had either A-8 or pocket 8s and had flopped a full house, putting him in control all along. But judging from his play, as we had seen it keenly for several hours, it did not seem likely that Tex would have raised before the flop with those hands. Neither was strong enough to raise from middle position. He probably would have only made a pre-flop call and possibly seen a raise to get a peek at the flop. Bumping it up like that jibed neither with the situation nor his style of play.

If our estimation of his not having A-8 or a pair of 8s was correct, then Tex could not, practically beyond a doubt, possess the winning hand. We knew this because my trip-aces with a queen kicker was the best hand, excluding the remote chance that Tex was drunk enough to have been sitting there the whole time with pocket deuces or 3s, either of which would now give him a winning full house. We'd arrived at that conclusion because Carla's and Preacher's hands had killed off all four kings, therefore, if Tex had an ace, his kicker could not beat my queen. If he didn't make the full house on the flop, he was just raising foolishly in the hope I might fold.

So I raised Tex back. He called with a drunken grunt, and thus we knew Tex had played his hand foolishly. We'd been able to capitalize on his shortcomings by using perfect signals to communicate the values of our hands. Tex's hand turned out to be A-J, and I took the huge pot with A-Q. Sayers and the Venezuelans, who had all been raised out of the pot, shot Tex a glance suggesting the displaced New Yorker ought to go back and try his luck in the Bronx.

Another hugely successful coup of collusion came when Carla made a king-high spade flush on the river. The signal we used to communicate flush draws was a simple continuation of the suited high-cards signal given after the deal: two chips lying neatly atop the cards. If the flop contained two cards of the right suit or all three to make the flush, the person among us with that hand would simply drop a third chip on top before removing all three.

Straight draws worked basically the same way, although by knowing the value of each person's hole cards we could deduce when a straight draw came alive simply by looking at the flop. In certain situations when the straight draw or made straight was not clear (middle and low straights), we would switch down to the bottom of the cards and place the chips in the location exactly opposite the flush signals. It was the same principle shifted into lower gear by using the entire backs of the cards for increased versatility.

Before Carla made her spade flush, we'd all known she had that draw. We also knew that her flush was the nuts, since Preacher, who had made a straight to the ace on the river, held the ace of spades in the hole. He had signalled us that information as soon as Carla signalled she had four cards to the flush after the flop. Merely by seeing two spades on board, Preacher knew that her potential flush was in spades. Therefore, he let us know that he had the ace of spades by tapping the top left corner of his hole cards in the "ace position." That little piece of info was crucial to the hand and ended up making us lots of extra money in the pot.

It had turned out that after the flop there were two lady players besides Carla chasing flushes. They both held two spades in the hole, though neither had a spade higher than the queen. But since one had also flopped top pair with her queen to go along with her flush draw, she bet out. The other had flopped a 9-8-7-6 *straight* flush draw, so she was locked in not only to call the bet but also to call all bets and raises to follow on the turn. Carla and Preacher were obligated to see the turn as well. Since Carla had the nut flush draw and Preacher would be needed for possible whipsawing, neither could fold his hand.

The turn card was not a spade but it gave the woman with the straight flush draw a straight to the 10. She bet it, possessing the nut hand for the moment, while Preacher, Carla and the other Venezuelan woman all called. Preacher had picked up a "gut" straight-to-the-ace draw, which gave us another collective out to win the pot on the river.

Since Carla's nut flush draw had been in spades, and Preacher's hand would win if he completed his straight and nobody made a flush, we had to be super aggressive even though the board pairing on the river, or just missing our straight and flush draws, would undoubtedly beat us. That's because the value of that fifth community card being any spade or the jack needed to fill Preacher's straight would bring a payoff greater than the odds against us winning the pot. In other words, it's like betting a horse at odds of 2 to 1 when the horse really has an even-money chance of winning the race. And to boot, we had the opportunity, should Carla hit her flush *and* Preacher his straight, of using Preacher as a re-raiser because his strong hand qualified for exposure at showdown after multiple raises. The only real way we could get wiped was if the board completely missed us on the river.

When the river brought another spade, we got a pleasant shock. Naturally Carla bet with her nut flush. We'd expected at least one of the Venezuelan women remaining in the pot to fold, since we couldn't know both had been chasing flush draws, and that one had already flopped top pair while the other turned a straight. But both called and set themselves up to be sandwiched between Carla and Preacher—the double-whammy Shangri-La utopia of collusion play.

They were obviously poor players, probably wealthy men's wives or mistresses, and with that last spade on board thought they had winning hands. But they were second and third best, and when they called Carla's bet, Preacher raised the pot, and when Carla re-raised, both women dumbly called again. They really got the brutal whipsawing and maybe even yelled at by their husbands.

There were also key situations when we whipsawed not to suck more money into the pot but rather to force players out of it. On one hand, Carla and I both picked up mid pocket pairs. Before the flop, another player raised. Preacher folded but Carla and I called. The flop presented a flush draw but did not help either of our hands. The raiser before the flop bet out; we called. The turn came a blank; the raiser checked as did we. Then when the river put a third club on board, the raiser came out betting. Carla raised him, then I quickly re-raised her with a blustery confidence meant to convey a sure winner.

The guy who'd raised initially and was now clamped in our vise chucked his hand. He obviously believed I had made the club-flush or determined that the double-raise was too much to justify calling. He must have also figured the possibility of Carla's capping the bet. But Carla folded her hand, so I was able to toss my unseen cards in the muck while taking the pot. I was pretty sure that the guy's hand sitting deeper in the muck was a higher pair than either Carla's or mine.

That hand was a classic example of the second means by which whipsawing makes winners of colluders. It drives players holding a better hand than yours out of the pot. In effect, that kind of whipsawing can be seen as super-power bluffing, sometimes called Black and Decker bluffing by those privy to the trade.

Believe it or not, after that night I did not cheat at poker again for more than two years. I never expected that I would, for poker cheating was not my forte, but something would come along that was too good to resist. It was a form of poker cheating that was unbelievable. I'll tell you about it later.

Other forms of signalling hands in live poker games

Most professional collusion teams use chips on cards to signal the value of their hands among its members. Not all of them, though, use the same method I keyed on with Preacher and Carla: placing chips on different spots of face-down cards. I have watched many teams at work and noted several derivatives of the chips-on-cards communication system.

Some teams, instead of using chips on cards, might just touch their cards in the same places I've mentioned to signal the corresponding hands. In situations where Preacher and Carla would have placed two chips on their pocket cards, someone using only fingers may simply tap the same spot twice with his index finger. If Preacher were holding A-K suited, he would place two chips on the top left corner of his cards, while a player with the "finger-tipping" team would simply fingertip the top left corner of his cards twice.

Whereas Preacher would show his A-K offsuit by sliding the top chip partially off the bottom one, the fingertipper would touch the same corner twice and then make a sliding gesture with his fingertip, identical in connotation to Preacher's sliding the top chip off the bottom one.

In comparing the two forms of subtle communication, I would say they're equally effective and each is about as undetectable as the other. I have picked up on teams using both systems over the years, though there can be no doubt that the chips-on-cards method is more in use.

Other teams use only stacks of chips to relay hole-card information to their players. They set the stacks up in certain formations, then change their appearance in accordance with hand values. For example, an initial bowling-pin 4-3-2-1 triangular stack formation changed into a 4-3-3 formation might mean that the player behind the chips is holding a high pair. Or if a block of 10 stacks originally containing 20 chips each now has a front stack shortened by five, this could signify a high-suited hand. Chip-stack signalling has many variances, although as a whole it is probably less dependable than chips on cards.

Another way for colluders to broadcast the value of their hands to one another is to do just that: audibly broadcast them. I'm not saying that Johnny will slam the poker table with a gavel and then announce, "Hear ye, hear ye! I have a pair of aces!" No, it will of course be a lot subtler than that. In fact, it will be so subtle that even someone looking to pick up on it would be hard pressed to catch it.

For example, a player asking the dealer to have a cocktail waitress sent over might be implicitly saying to his partner across the table that he has flopped both a straight and a flush draw. Then, reminding the dealer a second time on the river might signify he's made the flush. As well, a player turning to his right-side neighbor and asking if he'd had any luck with his last keno ticket might be telling the player to the neighbor's right that he wants him to re-raise every time he raises for the duration of the pot.

Collusion languages go on and on and can seem as easy or as complex as Esperanto. The main criteria for developing them is truly knowing your partners and studying their natural ways of speech. The most difficult part of the actual language communication designed to divulge hands is avoiding the pitfall of giving hand-value signals by accident. Since language collusion must sound completely natural, then obviously certain common phrases with hidden poker meanings will oftentimes come up—and not only from your collusion mates. Someone else at the table may say something like, "I can't stand all the smoke in here!" That very phrase might be your signal to raise, and if a lapse of concentration occurs whereby a collusion teammate raises the pot when neither of you have a hand, it will cost you money and later on grief.

The risk of miscommunication is the primary reason why most experienced teams adapt to signalling using chips and cards. Some teams might use only chips and build certain chips-on-table formations that communicate the hands. Others might use an imaginary card on the table, something like a four-lined rectangle, perhaps bigger than a real card as to reduce the chances of bad chip placement. My final point about team collusion is that there are so many different ways to implement the signalling of hands that they could by themselves fill up an entire dictionary.

Mucking and switching cards

Physical cheating in poker rooms is much less common than collusion but it does go on, and when it does the thievery is much more pronounced. There are several methods of "active" cheating, the most common of which are marking cards, crimping cards and even switching cards. And in some cases—it happens more often than you might think—poker dealers in the most reputable cardrooms are right in the thick of it, usually in a partnership with one or more players at their table.

Let's start with switching cards. This is a highly effective cheating technique that when implemented by real pros removes most of the honest players at the table from their money. It is typically executed by a pair of skilled card-muckers (those able to palm cards and move them in and out of play), although I have seen it done by threesomes and amateurs alike. The key is that the muckers have to be seated next to one another. To give you a good example of a card-switching team at work, I will recount an experience I had at the Bicycle Club in Bell Gardens, California, in 2002.

During my 25-year career cheating casinos, I often took breaks where I spent a lot of down time playing poker. I liked playing in California more than Las Vegas. The action in the giant card clubs in and around LA attracted much more loose money and less skilled players than did the casino cardrooms in Vegas. I would go play poker in California four or five times a year, usually for about a week each time. And when I did, cheating was the furthest thing on my mind.

But not on everybody else's.

On a beautiful Saturday afternoon that summer, I strolled into the Bicycle Club after a brisk four-hour drive across the desert from Vegas. My favorite game was $20–40 hold'em. As I'd anticipated for a Saturday afternoon, there was a waiting list to get into the game. They had eight tables going at my desired limits and two-dozen names before mine on the list.

All of us travelling poker players know how good the food is in the Bicycle Club coffee shop. I wandered inside it and enjoyed a Belgian waffle topped with whipped cream and strawberries. When I came back onto the cardroom floor, there were still several names before mine on the list, so I hung back on the rail and watched the action.

I began by casually observing a $20–40 game just below me. It was a typical loose-action table evenly populated by Asians and Caucasians. I happened to love playing with Asians because of their loose style of play. Very seldom did you have a "dead game" when Chinese and Filipinos were at the table. Wild action and reckless gambling were in their blood.

Suddenly my attention was drawn to another $20–40 hold'em game one table deeper into the casino. What first attracted me to it was a movement barely perceptible to my senses. I may not have been an experienced poker cheat, but I was still one of the best all-around casino cheaters in business, and I could sniff out cheating like an airport dog did the scent of marijuana. After all, cheating is cheating, and many of its poker forms spilled over into blackjack, roulette and craps.

The movement that shifted my gander was a very subtle one, perhaps too subtle to escape my peripheral vision. The table I was now watching was spread lengthways in front of me. In two seats across the table from the dealer, their backs to me, sat a man in a baseball cap and a woman with medium-length dark hair. The man was seated to the woman's left. Neither one was dressed obtrusively; they blended in perfectly with the other players at their table, and with most everyone else in the card club. To everyone's eyes but mine, their actions warranted no double takes.

What I noticed first was that the man's right shoulder and the woman's left shoulder bobbed simultaneously. It was the slightest movement but somehow it caught my attention. Out

of curiosity, not really thinking something was up, I continued watching. After the flop, the man folded and the woman
stayed in the hand. From where I stood I couldn't see the
community cards on the table, but I could tell who was playing and who was not. The woman chucked her hand in the
muck after someone bet on the turn.

I saw the dealer sweep the pot to the eventual winner, then
watched him deal the next hand. As soon as I determined that
the couple had received their cards for the new hand, I put
my sights on them closely. At that instant, their shoulders
bobbed again. The man put in a pre-flop raise while the
woman folded. I watched a pretty decent pot unfold, and
when it was over the dealer slid him the chips.

The third time I saw their shoulders bob told me they were
cheating. To confirm my suspicions I decided to make a pass
of their table. On the next deal, I descended the steps and
headed directly toward the couple's rear. As they were receiving their second cards, I slipped right up behind them. I
froze for an instant to get a good peek, and my growing curiosity, which was rapidly turning into fascination, was not
disappointed. In that split second, and I mean *split*, the man
and woman exchanged a card. It was one of the deftest movements I had ever seen, and, believe me, I had seen many,
scores of which originated from Yours Truly.

With a bare minimum of shoulder and arm movement, the
man using his right hand, the woman her left, each palmed a
card and slid his wrist along the table toward the other. The
length of their arms served to hide the action from the dealer
and other players at the table. It simply blocked everyone's
view as the man dropped off his card and scooped up the
woman's and vice-versa. And, for added protection, they
used their bent free arms to create a barrier against anyone
who might have a side view. It took me a few more episodes

of this to see how truly gifted they were, but I surely enjoyed the show.

I wanted to see more of it. When my name was finally announced for an open seat, I was disappointed not to be led to that particular table. The table I was assigned to play at was two tables away from the cheaters. In spite of the fact that I found myself at a great-action loose game filled with Asians, I immediately summoned the floorman and put in for a table change. When he asked if I had a preference, I indicated the one I had been watching from the rail. I just hoped that the cheating couple would still be at that table by the time a seat on it opened up for me. I knew from cheater's experience that people with a dishonest edge at gambling did not like to hang around too long in one place, no matter how opportune the situation.

To my delight, the couple was still playing when the floorman escorted me to their table. He sat me down in the first seat to the dealer's left. I was directly across from the cheaters, a prime spot for viewing. I now noticed that the woman was wearing dark glasses. At first I thought that was foolish, that wearing sunglasses would draw attention to her. However, on looking around the poker room I saw at least two people at each table wearing shades. In fact, I regretted that I didn't have similar glasses to conceal my eyes. I didn't want this couple noticing how interested I was in their game. I didn't want to spook them.

The first hand I watched them play closeup, they both threw their cards in the muck. I took that to mean that even with all four cards they couldn't make a single playable hand. At the same time, I realized how powerful their scam was. Say, for instance, the man was dealt A-7 offsuit and the woman A-6 offsuit. Neither of these is really a playable hand, especially from early position. But if the man were able to slip the woman his ace in exchange for her 6, she would then have the A-A monster that poker players like to call "American Airlines." The man could then fold his 7-6 and relax while watching his partner play the big hand. The same could be done to create nut flush and straight draws. If between their four cards they could find an A-K suited, voila! And sometimes one of them all by his lonesome would pick up that dynamite hand so they wouldn't need to switch.

The next hand they went into action, just as if some director seated high above yelled out that very word. I timed my glance at them so it would pick up their move without lingering. I watched the woman receive her second card and the man his a split second later. There was a tiny hesitation before their shoulders bobbed and their hands and arms jerked ever so slightly. By moving their heads while shifting backward, they'd stolen a glance at each other's cards. Then they made an instantaneous decision as to which cards to switch, and followed through. It was all lightning quick.

My hand was marginally playable but I threw it in the muck as soon as the action was on me. I just wanted to watch the couple. Instinctively I knew they were a top-notch cheating team, and of course I appreciated their display of talent. I had always harbored a great respect for those with both the balls and intelligence to successfully cheat at gambling. It may have been true that this couple was cheating the players and not the house, but in no way did that reality lessen their skill.

The flop on that hand came K-9-8 with flush possibilities. However, when the woman raised the initial bettor, I doubted she was chasing a flush. I secretly put her on at least a pair of kings and maybe even trips. Her partner folded his hand and lightly feigned disgust.

A queen came on the turn, followed by a 4 on the river.

There were no possible straights or flushes. The woman bet out, got called and won the pot. What did she reveal at showdown? You guessed it: a black pair of kings to form a set.

I stayed at that table until they left two hours later. They really cleaned up the game, $1,500 profit between them, two-thirds of it going to the woman. And I'm sure they exercised some restraint. They simply could not show strong pocket pairs every time they entered a pot; that would be suspicious. Members of any successful casino cheating team knew that their actual grifting skills were only part of it. Every facet of their operation, from approach to the table to execution of cheating techniques to cashing out and leaving the cardroom, had to be fine-tuned. Many very talented teams got busted or ruined because of weakness in areas that had nothing to do with actual cheating—mainly greed and infighting among the members.

You may now be asking yourself some questions about the experience I just shared with you. One of them must surely be: okay, if this couple was so good that they were able to avoid detection at the table, then how come the surveillance cameras above didn't catch them?

It's a good question but easy to answer. The first thing to know about casino surveillance anywhere, whether it is in Las Vegas's super megaresort casinos or in the smallest Colorado cardrooms, is that cameras only *record* the action. They are not capable of picking up a telephone, dialing the number of the casino floor and saying to a floorman, "Listen, Charlie, you see that couple sitting in seats 5 and 6 at table 3? They're switching cards." No, it doesn't work that way. Someone on the floor, or—more rarely—someone actually watching from the eye in the sky above, has got to see the cheating action take place, and then shift the cameras into the right angle to film the cheating action in question.

Another thing to remember about casino surveillance, and this holds especially true in Las Vegas, Atlantic City and most other major gambling areas, is that surveillance people are less interested in watching poker games and catching poker cheats than they are in keeping the main casino under relentless watch. Many surveillance chiefs in the gambling world will tell you this is not so, but they're full of it. Why? Because people cheating in poker rooms are not costing the casinos any money. It's the players who are getting ripped off. Any undetected poker cheating does not have the result of hurting the casino's bottom line (unless the dealer is stealing rake money). Do you really think that Steve Wynn or Sheldon Adelson or even Becky Binion of the Horseshoe is as worried for poker players as they are for their own casinos? Me, I doubt it.

This is not to say that camera surveillance of poker rooms is lax or unimportant. I'm only saying what I know to be reality as far as game protection is concerned. In 25 years of cheating casinos throughout the world, I never, not *one* time, was back-roomed or questioned about something coming out of the eye in the sky. I must have done 10,000 illicit casino moves in my lifetime, and never has a surveillance operator seen one and reported it down to the floor. So if a good poker cheating team can keep floorpeople in the dark, they can keep those working in surveillance rooms oblivious to their moves.

During my years as a part-time poker player and cheater, I have stumbled across a handful of card-switching teams plying their trade. I saw that couple from the Bicycle Club on two other occasions. One was at the Bellagio in Las Vegas, which proved they were capable of doing their act underneath the best surveillance equipment and personnel in the world. The other was at the Taj Majal in Atlantic City, the Boardwalk's number-one poker destination, at least in terms of volume.

I have seen different mucking teams working poker tables in the Caribbean as well as in London's poker-famed Victoria Club. I even witnessed a three-man team (actually it was a two-woman-one-man affair) switching cards among themselves in Costa Rica, and, lo and behold, I saw the man playing in the 2003 World Series of Poker championship event! He did rather well, though I must tell you that during the hour I watched him, he did not dare switch any cards. Naturally cheating of that nature would not be on display in an event so severely scrutinized, nor would it be easy to find yourself at the same table with your partner sitting next to you.

But don't get me wrong. A lot of major cheating goes on at the major poker tournaments, including the World Series of Poker (WSOP), but card-switching is not something likely to happen there. I will talk about tournament cheating consortiums in a later chapter.

Marking cards

Now let's move on to marking cards in public cardrooms. This method of cheating is about as old as the game itself. It has taken on many forms, some of them crude and amateurish, others highly sophisticated, and one, in which I had the challenge and pleasure to participate, so unbelievably advanced I would have to call it one of the greatest gambling scams I've ever seen, and that statement coming from me means something.

I will not waste your precious reading time presenting too much material on the low-level card-crimpers and card-scratchers out there. Most of these people, seemingly more often women than men, get caught before the next shuffle. Before they're even taken to the back room, their pointy fingernails are already damaged, which adds to the evidence against them.

What these low-level cheaters usually do is put creases, crimps or scratches on the backs of aces, kings and queens, mostly ignoring the rest of the deck. The markings are obvious, and surveillance routinely spots the culprits in all corners of cardrooms, although their preferred workplace seems to be hold'em games. Not that it's more effective to mark cards at hold'em tables than at other games, but rather that hold'em is by far the most popular form of poker. As that popularity continues to spread, cheaters will keep pursuing the best opportunities for making cash.

Those card-altering players not discovered by surveillance are often found out when you detect their work on your cards. You notice a mark on the card when the light hits it a certain way, or sometimes the indentation is so bold it glows in the dark. Whenever this happens you can either ask for a deck-change or just get up and play at another table.

People tampering with the cards will stop doing so once a new deck is demanded by another player at the table. If you really want to rattle an incompetent card-marker, just say this to the floorman as a request to get the cards changed: "There's something fishy about the backs of these cards." You might notice someone jump out of the game as if his chair caught fire. In short, card-markers get spooked at poker tables faster than prairie dogs do at the onset of a solar eclipse.

Not so, however, with the real pros. I'm talking about the genuine artists, "daubers" who paint the cards with a special solution that is visible only to those wearing special glasses or contact lenses made for that purpose. Even that form of card-marking is no longer the most advanced. The true Picassos and Rembrandts of today's card-marking scams use paint that's even better than plain old invisible; it disappears and leaves not the slightest trace.

Let me tell you an incredible story that took place in the

late 1990s. At the time, I was working the casinos with my partner, Pat, whom you might have seen profiled with me on Challenge TV's *The World's Greatest Gambling Scams*. He was dating this chick, Dawn, who claimed to know a New York optometrist looking to market a new invisible card-marking solution to the highest bidder among casino cheaters. At first I was uninterested. I had known about most card-marking schemes for years, and those I was unfamiliar with I'd seen in the movies. But when Pat relayed to me what Dawn had told him and sworn to be true, I got interested real quickly.

Supposedly the optometrist's invisible card-marking solution disappeared from the cards 30 minutes after its application. That blew my mind. The first thing I thought of was how perfect that amount of time would be. One of the earliest rules my mentor had taught me about casino cheating was to never overexpose yourself or your cheating methods. If you're marking cards in a poker game, you don't want to sit there more than a half hour anyway. The best course to embark on was to hit a table for that limited amount of time and then boogie, regardless of the amount of profits. What could be better than having your evidence disappear from the cards at the same time you disappear from the table?

Not much.

I ended up suspending all my casino operations to make a foray into poker cheating by way of marking the cards. I hadn't been involved in poker cheating for a while and didn't really want to get back into it, but I was keen on seeing if the optometrist's product really worked.

The solution was very expensive, five grand for a little perfume-sample-size bottle that contained enough of the stuff to mark the aces and picture cards of about a hundred decks. Dawn and Pat tried to convince me to buy two bottles before seeing that the solution really worked. Dawn vouched for the optometrist and Pat vouched for Dawn, so I took the shot. But I was afraid I'd be shelling out 10 grand for two bottles of piss, so I ordered only one.

The optometrist had first developed special contact lenses needed to see the marks on the cards. Optical devices (mainly glasses) used in card-marking schemes were nothing new. But what made this scam so appealing was that the solution disappeared so rapidly. To my knowledge, that technical improvement was revolutionary at the time. I had a friend who worked in casino surveillance and he had never heard of it. His ignorance was good enough for me.

Back then I was still living in Las Vegas. Wiring the money was out of the question, so I stuck five grand in cash inside a magazine that I stuffed into a Fedex envelope. I shipped the package off to the optometrist in New York and waited. A week later I received five pair of the contact lenses, the bottle of solution and a note informing me that reorders were only available in the same $5,000 increments. He also wished me a lot of luck.

I was pumped up by enthusiasm for this new venture. No later than 15 minutes after the packet's arrival, Dawn, Pat and I popped in the lenses. It took us a few minutes to get used to them in our eyes, during which I gathered a deck of cards and spread them on the coffee table. My living room took on a dull light green hue, and it seemed a little grainy, almost as though I were looking through a night scope.

Of course I had absolutely no experience with marking cards, so I applied common sense. I knew from reading books that cards were usually marked in the center of their backs. Card cheats marked in that fashion because the corners of cards were always being damaged by player-mishandling and dealer-shuffling, while the middle part of cards usually stayed intact. Since Dawn had said that only a small dab was necessary, I wouldn't overdo it. I unscrewed the little tube, and using a cotton swab dabbed a small amount of the solution onto the backs of a few cards. I also took a good whiff of the solution to see if it had any smell. Invisible and disappearing card-marking solution wouldn't do any good if it stunk up the cardroom.

We waited anxiously for the markings to appear. But nothing was immediately discernible on the cards. I rapidly got the feeling of being had, but then suddenly a very pale bluish-greenish tinge appeared and took form on the cards. It looked like a small fingerprint. We stared down at the cards in disbelief, as if observing a butterfly somehow turning back into a caterpillar.

We kept the lenses in our eyes and waited for the solution to disappear. After just a few minutes it became fainter; 20 minutes later it was completely gone.

I was in shock. The ramifications of such a device were insane.

I gave a final rub over the cards with my index finger to make sure there were no remnants of the solution sensitive to touch. If there had been, the scam would have proved useless. But they remained as smooth as the rest of the unmarked cards in the deck. Fundamentally, the contact lenses and the solution were sound. The only problems to deal with were those of transporting the solution to the poker tables and its application to the cards.

Dawn greatly simplified matters when she volunteered to be part of the actual operation when it was carried out. Being a woman naturally gave her feminine advantages. She already had the handbag filled with cosmetic cases and other items women routinely store inside it. No reason why she couldn't be looking into her little pocket mirror while on the poker table, dabbing on some rouge or tying back her hair.

While ostensibly performing such innocuous gestures, Dawn could work the solution onto her fingertips and mark the cards as she picked them up off the deal.

We decided to test the operation in California. We drove to the Commerce casino, another giant poker club not far from the Bicycle Club. Dawn proved to be real cool under pressure. It had turned out that she was a scammer her whole life who had been involved in a major roulette-wheel-clocking team that had beat casinos in Europe for a sizeable chunk of cash. Back now in California, she marked the cards like a real pro. Her movements were naturally feminine and she didn't go into her handbag more often than the other women at the table. I intently observed the players at the table and cardroom personnel. No one gave Dawn a second look.

We had all been wearing the contact lenses on entering the casino. Within 15 minutes, Dawn had marked two aces and three kings that had come her way during the deals, and they lit up like fireworks displays in our eyes. We didn't concentrate too much on the playing of hands, however. We just wanted to test the lenses and the solution in a live game.

Twenty minutes later we got out of the game. I then did a walk-by half an hour later to verify that the markings on the cards had disappeared. The same blue-backed deck of cards was in play, or so I thought, and I delighted in the fact that none of the cards face down on the table had remnants of the markings.

But then with a start I realized that the woman dealing was not the one who'd been dealing when we left the game. I suddenly remembered that poker dealers rotate from table to table every half hour or 40 minutes. They bring and remove their personal trays containing chips and two decks of cards, one red-backed and the other blue-backed, which meant the marked deck was no longer in play. I couldn't verify that

Dawn's markings had thoroughly disappeared. We would have to take it for granted that they did.

Later on in the hotel room, I tested the process repeatedly on decks we'd bought in the gift shop. Each time, the markings were completely obliterated within the allotted 30 minutes.

But there were several difficulties with this immense scam that had to be ironed out. The first problem I became aware of was that the half-hour window between marking the decks and seeing the solution disappear was not long enough to afford us any substantial playing time with the compromised cards. It would take Dawn that whole 30 minutes to see enough hands where she could mark a significant number of the high-valued cards. Foolishly, I had not thought of that before. It was necessary to find a way to get a greater number of cards marked in a shorter period of time, so as to give us enough time to rake in a few pots before the markings started disappearing.

Well, as foolish as my oversight may have been, the solution to our problem was equally simple. We only had to give Dawn some help with marking the cards. Pat and I would have to apply the solution to the cards we'd be dealt as well. Though that appeared to be somewhat more challenging from a male perspective, in practice it was hardly difficult at all. We just padded the insides of cigarette packs with the solution and rubbed our fingertips in it as we removed a cigarette.

For Pat this came as easy as riding a bicycle. He'd been a chain smoker for 20 years. But I had never smoked a cigarette in my life. I was totally uncomfortable handling a cigarette pack, even if the chore were only to legitimately remove a cigarette. However, when there's a will there's a way. I had faced many inherent obstacles in the life of a professional cheat and had overcome all of them. This one would be no more daunting as long as I developed confidence and practiced the craft, as I had so diligently practiced my pastposting moves.

We returned to the Commerce a week later. We patiently waited until all three of us got into the same $3–6 hold'em game. Best, I'd decided, was to start in a low-stakes game. The attending floormen were generally less attentive since low-limit players had fewer problems and got involved in fewer arguments than high-limit players. I took notice that the particular floorman here was a young bucko named Gordon who comically resembled the ex-football great Gordon Banks in his early days.

We didn't start marking the cards until a new dealer came on the game, which assured us of an uninterrupted half hour of play with the same deck, unless, of course, a player requested a deck change. The table was full. I was in Seat 3, the third player to the left of the dealer. Pat occupied Seat 5 and Dawn was in Seat 8. However, position was of no importance in this kind of operation. We could have also used collusion in order to strengthen the power of our operation that much more, but it was foolhardy to risk taking heat for repetitive raising while running a scam far more sophisticated and at the same time much more dangerous.

After 15 minutes at the table, we had all four aces marked, one king, three of the queens, three jacks and all the 10s. The markings themselves distinguished which cards were which. Similar to the chip-placements on the cards used in the collusion scam, we marked the aces on the left of the card slightly above center, the kings on the right of the card slightly above center, the queens on the left of the card slightly below center and the jacks on the right of the card slightly below center. In staying near the center of the cards, we avoided the markings being damaged by players and dealers handling them.

We had a solid 15 minutes to play hands before the solution began disappearing. The first hand we won with the help of the paint belonged to Dawn, who happened to be an excellent legitimate poker player as well. She limped into the hand with a pair of 4s on the small blind, even though she saw that a player behind her had pocket 10s and was sure to raise. When you know what cards your opponent has in the hole, you can play extremely loose and call virtually every hand before the flop. The idea is to get into as many pots as possible and then hang around to the river only when you know your hand is best. You never have to bluff.

The flop came 9-4-3 with two hearts. A woman in early position whose cards were not marked bet $3. Dawn called, Pat and I folded, and the man with the pocket 10s naturally raised. Both the woman and Dawn called. We knew about the man's overpair (pocket pair higher than all three community cards) but could only guess what the woman was playing. We figured she either had a pair of 9s or flopped a heart flush draw.

The turn came J♦. The woman checked, and the man with the 10s bet $6. Dawn knew her trip-4s had the guy beat but she couldn't be sure what the woman had. She decided her best move was to call. If she raised, the guy might chuck his hand, thinking Dawn had paired with the jack on board.

The river card was the 8♥. The man quickly let out a false tell. His hand made a sudden movement to his chips as though he were anxious to bet. His ploy was to make his two opponents think that the eight on the river gave him either a straight or a flush. The woman, possibly maneuvered by the guy's action, checked. The man followed through on his bluff and bet the $6. Even though we did not mark suits on the backs of high cards, Dawn was certain the man could have neither a straight nor a flush, since he had a pair of 10s and thus only one could be a heart. With that knowledge she was able to raise. The woman folded and the man called. The dealer pushed the pot to Dawn.

We played five more hands before the half hour was up. We only won one, but more importantly was the money saved by not chasing better hands to the river. As much as you win pots by knowing your opponents cards, you know when the time's right to fold your own. On one hand I had pocket kings and I was sitting on the button, a great starting situation all around. Of course I re-raised the pot after the player before me raised with A-Q. When the flop came A-Q-3, I knew it was time to muck my kings.

After that session we met up at our hotel down the road. We discussed what had happened and what improvements we could make. There had been only one major problem. On numerous hands, players receiving their cards laid their chips directly over the markings. Again this was an unforeseen problem. You just could never have everything covered when you embarked on new cheating operations. Each one always turned out more complicated than you had envisioned.

To rectify the problem, I suggested we mark the backs of the cards a little higher and lower than we'd been doing, since those players who covered their hole cards with chips placed them smack on the middle more often than not. When we put the adjustment into practice, the results were immediately favorable—90% of the markings were not obscured by players' chips or anything else they laid on top of their hole cards.

Besides that, everything had gone smoothly. None of us had experienced difficulty while marking the cards and, as far as I could see, we hadn't taken any heat. Nobody seemed to know we'd been together.

We agreed we were ready to up the ante. When we returned to the casino after lunch, we headed directly for the $20–40 tables. We also determined it was not necessary for us all to play at the same table. Since the three of us were competent poker players, each would have the stone-cold nuts on his side by reading the paint. Besides, having to wait to secure three seats at the same table was cumbersome and risked taking heat when floorpeople noticed we liked playing together.

I, as leader of our team, would have to be extra sharp with internal security. By spreading out we widened our playing field, which in turn increased the chances of detection. All you had to do was the math. If you're cheating three tables at once, your chances of encountering problems are three times greater. The one caution I did give Dawn and Pat was to occasionally throw a hand. It wouldn't look right if every time we called someone's hand we won. The best cover we could give ourselves was to play a few hands as if we didn't know what cards our opponents were holding.

We played all afternoon and suffered not the least misfortune. It was truly one of the most amazing episodes I have ever witnessed in my casino-cheating career. Of course I had worried about a squadron of armed security guards grabbing me right off the game, yanking the pack of cigarettes off the table, plucking the green-tinted contacts out of my eyes and finally shipping all that evidence off to the prosecutor's office. But none of that ever happened. And it probably never would as long as we conducted ourselves intelligently and never became too greedy.

But marking cards at poker tables was not my true calling. While with Preacher and Carla I had wrestled with the morality of cheating the players instead of the house. My private little war had always been against the casinos, especially in Las Vegas. That's where my juice was; that's what I really lived for. So after just a few months of the card-marking operation, I returned to my old casino partners and went back to beating the traditional casino games.

Are these kinds of high-tech card-marking scams going on today? You bet. And the equipment, mainly the marking solution and the contact lenses, is even better today. I'm not saying that cheaters are running around with lasers to mark the cards and computer chips in their eyes to see the paint, but I am telling you that organized teams are still out there looking right through your hole cards.

When Dawn, Pat and I broke off that operation, Dawn went out on her own. I've been told she's still marking cards in poker rooms everywhere. I've also learned that the optometrist who invented the solution had over the years sold hundreds of bottles of the stuff. I don't know how many different teams or individuals were in the market for his product, but I can say that those who were have used it without running into major problems. I know this for two reasons. One is that no one has ever been arrested by gaming authorities anywhere for using a marking solution that disappears. Had this ever happened, it would have been major news and blown through the gaming industry with gales the strength of those whipped up by former Nevada Gaming Control Board agent Ron Harris when he got busted for rigging keno games in Atlantic City.

The other reason is that my friend who still works in the surveillance room of a major Las Vegas casino has never heard of any investigations into related matters, nor has his casino ever received any warnings from Griffin Investigations, a private detective agency which serves as a watchdog for US casinos, that these kinds of card-markers are in town.

One can also speculate that the New York optometrist was not the only clever person to develop invisible-disappearing paint to mark cards with. He was most likely the first, but I imagine a fair number of others have come up with similar solutions being used in cardrooms today.

It is also highly possible that disappearing paint is not completely foreign to the tables of major poker tournaments. Imagine the edge this form of cheating brings to no-limit tournaments. Just about every other hand at the final table you see someone pushing all-in with huge stacks of chips. Lots of these moves are bluffs. Bluffing tactics are a major strategy intrinsic to big-time pot and no-limit poker tournaments. Often the players doing the pushing have jack shit and are simply trying to drive the opposition out of the pot. But if a player sitting on the other side of those stacks being pushed his way knows what the pusher's hole cards are, it's all over; he can't be beat.

I personally have no evidence of successful major tournament players using a solution similar to the one supplied by the optometrist, but if I were a *legitimate* betting man, I would certainly lay odds that some of them have bottles of the stuff in their medicine cabinets as we speak.

How do you defend yourself against this kind of operation aimed at you? You don't. My best advice here is to pay attention to the players who are consistently beating you or just plain winning at your table. If they seem to have a knack of making the right calls and lay-downs, you might be in against someone marking the cards you hold in your hand. It's probably best to bail out and find somewhere else to play. The chances of your leaving one crooked game to land in another are remote.

Okay, you might have a problem with that. I know. You're really comfortable in your game and don't want to go. You want to know for sure if the guy who's made five correct calls in a row is marking the cards. Well, forget about trying to spot the contact lenses in his eyes or feeling the cards he may have marked. The lenses I wore to read card-markings were tinted only slightly green. They were no more obvious than those you see in the eyes of beautiful women.

Nowadays colored contact lenses are about as popular as skin tone products. How many women do you know who prefer brown eyes to light blue or green? Plus the lenses used for reading cards today are even less phony looking. So, believe me, you're not going to extract any information by peering into the eyes of a player rousing your suspicions. And you're not going to gain anything by searching out the cards themselves for evidence. Cheaters pay big money for their cheating devices. They're not about to leave you clues so, like I said, anytime you suspect someone at your table is cheating, not only by way of marking cards, your safest bet is to bring whatever chips you have left to another table. Before they disappear, too.

Dealer and player cheating partnerships

Let us not forget that public cardroom poker dealers are human beings, too. They are not dealing machines with slots above their breasts for your tokes (tips). They live, breathe and enjoy themselves as much as everyone they deal cards to at their tables. Likewise, they have the same problems, feelings of depression and crushed dreams that their players often do. So what does this all mean?

It means that poker dealers are no more or less inclined to be dishonest than poker players. It's all a matter of situation and circumstance. If a poker dealer gets into a financial jam, one of the ways to resolve it might be to steal money on the job. After all, if clerks steal from the register and bookkeepers fudge the books, why should we not expect dealers under pressure to do the same? And if they wanted to steal money, they'd have the advantage that no money would be missing after they've stolen it.

In my many casino-jaunts across the world, I witnessed

and even met dealers in business for themselves. Not only at poker but in casino table games as well. One of these affable dealer-cheaters was a handsome kid named Effie from Aruba. He was one of the Arubans involved in a passing-off-chips scam that benefited my casino team in the eighties. After that profitable partnership we became friends. I would call him each time I went to Aruba and we'd get together and go clubbing. He turned me on to some of the island's friendliest women.

Ten years after I met him, Effie told me he had a friend from Aruba who'd become a naturalized American in Atlantic City and got hired as a poker dealer at the Taj Mahal casino, which ran the resort gambling town's number-one poker room. He also let me know that "Bobby likes to do business on the side."

I promised Effie I'd look up Bobby the next time I went to Atlantic City. That turned out to be seven months later and I kept my promise. I found Bobby dealing a juicy $30–60 seven-card stud game on the swing shift. He had a similar appearance to his friend back in Aruba, the same soft but chiselled features. I approached Bobby subtly on his break and we agreed to meet on the boardwalk after his shift.

"So you're a friend of Effie's," Bobby said in his soothing Aruban accent mixed with a laugh. "I bet you got rich with him."

That was all I needed to hear. Now I wanted to see how I'd get rich with Bobby. The answer was not long in forthcoming. The simple fact that Effie sent me to see Bobby spared both of us the you-can't-trust-me-I-can't-trust-you bullshit.

"Here's what you do," Bobby said to me as we leaned over the boardwalk railing and peered out into the dark ocean. "Take a seat in my game as soon as you can but not before midnight."

"When does your shift tomorrow start?" I asked.

"Eight o'clock. Don't worry. We'll have four hours. That's plenty of time to make a little money." He laughed and we clinked our paper cups filled with beer.

Bobby had not bothered telling me what he would do. He only wanted to know if I was adept at receiving signals. I told him that giving and receiving signals in casinos and card-rooms had been my business for nearly 20 years. He explained that he, not I, would be doing the signalling. There would only be four signals: fold, call, bet, and raise. All I had to do is follow them every hand, Bobby guaranteed, and we would "make out like bandits."

The signals were easy enough and well concealed. Each was given by the slightest movement of his thumb as he held the deck. When he wanted me to fold, Bobby's thumb would hang by half its width off the front of the deck. When he wanted me to call, his thumb would slide back onto the top of the deck and a little to the left. A raise he indicated by moving his thumb slightly farther down but still to the left. When the pot was either checked to me or I was first to act, and Bobby wanted me to bet, he would flash me the same signal he used to indicate a call. To give his signalling camouflage he constantly varied the position of his thumb on top of the deck. He would do that even when I was out of the hand.

The next night I showed up at the Taj Mahal poker room at 11:30. I spotted Bobby dealing his $30–60 stud game, although it was one table away from the one he'd been dealing at the night before. The table was full and there were two names ahead of mine on the list. I figured my timing was right and that I would get a seat on Bobby's table just after midnight.

I actually had to wait until 12:30, at which time I nestled comfortably into Seat 3, the third spot to Bobby's left. I posted my ante and got right into the flow of the game. The first four hands Bobby flashed me the fold signal, his thumb slightly off the pack of cards. On the fifth hand he had me call. My door card was the 10♠. I had A♠-K♠ in the hole. I did not think it was a coincidence that Bobby had me call with my first strong starting hand, three royal flush connectors. Somehow he knew what my hole cards were.

On fourth street the player in Seat 1 paired up with 8s. He checked to Player 2, who checked to me. I had received the J♣, giving me four cards to an ace-high straight and still three to a royal flush. I glanced at Bobby's hand holding the deck. His thumb was now squarely on the pack and to the left. He was telling me to bet. I bet $30. Player 4 on my left raised. Player 7, who'd picked up a pair of 7s on board, called, as did Players 1 and 2. Bobby had me call the raise.

On fifth street I received another good card: the J♥. This gave me a pair of jacks on board with a gut ace-high straight draw. Bobby again gave me the signal to bet, so I cut $60 in red $5 chips into three stacks in front of me. Player 4, the previous raiser, now folded. Player 7 called. Player 1 called, then Player 2 threw his cards in the muck.

Sixth street brought me the 6♠, adding an ace-king-high flush draw to my possibilities. I was still high on board. I received the bet signal and obliged, 60 bucks more into the pot. Players 7 and 1 called, and the dealer heaped everyone's chips into the pot at the middle of the table.

Seventh street down and dirty gave me the monster card: Q♠. I had an ace-king-queen-high flush. About the only way I was losing that hand was if someone bought a full house. Bobby had me check. I guessed he was baiting someone to bet so I could raise. The guy in Seat 7 with his matching 7s on board suddenly bet out. I noticed he had three clubs to go with them. Player 1 folded.

I had my hands on my stack ready to raise, but suddenly I

noticed that Bobby's thumb had dipped off the cards. This meant he wanted me to fold. He was telling me to junk my ace-high flush, which would beat any club-flush Player 7 might have had. I couldn't imagine that he'd made a full boat, although I was fairly certain Bobby had not mixed up his signals and that I had read him correctly. I forced myself not to make eye contact with him as that might alert other astute players to something going on between us.

I tossed my hand. The guy sure as hell did make the full house, and he was one of those players who felt obliged to show it to the whole table. He was not required to since there were no callers, but he cockily flopped over three big 9s. He had 9s in the hole from the start and bought the third one down and dirty.

I played at Bobby's table until five o'clock in the morning. Bobby checked out at four but I wanted to stay and show that last hour of action to quell any suspicions that may have arisen. That because I won $2,500 during Bobby's hours. On the relief dealer's stints, I played without the help and held my own.

The scam had worked like a charm. Bobby guided me through each and every hand I was dealt. He had me call a few losers but that was only to keep the cover. I won just about every significant pot I was in at showdown. Naturally I figured out what Bobby's angle was but I couldn't figure how he was doing it. There was no doubt in my mind he knew everyone's hole cards in the hands he had me play in. That was his gig, and it was huge.

I met up again with Bobby on the boardwalk. It was dawn. We cut up the profits and then had a coffee together as we watched the sun come up over the ocean. Bobby exhibited no compunction telling me how he did it, only because I had proved myself such an adroit cheating partner.

"It was really quite simple," he said with an easy laugh," and he qualified that by telling me he knew a handful of Atlantic City dealers working the same scam. "All I do is gather the face-up cards the way I'm supposed to, and when I need more cards I just take a peek at a few of the face-down ones. Then when I shuffle up the cards for the next deal, I make sure not to disturb the clump containing those cards at the top of the deck. As you might not have noticed, I'm pretty good at fake shuffles and fake cuts. So you see, by remembering the order of the cards I picked up and how many hands I'm dealing in the next round, I can keep track of everyone's hole cards. Then I just play your hand with that knowledge. As long as you don't blow the signals, we get the money. There's nothing more to it."

Maybe so, but this was one of the simplest yet most devastatingly effective methods of dealer-collusion cheating I'd ever seen. Plus it was essentially undetectable. When you have a collusion scam with the dealer at its helm, you have tremendous odds in your favor, and at the same time the player-partner is virtually immune to errors and detection by the rest of the table. Furthermore, the cheater's cards always appear normal and above suspicion; it's not like he's being dealt an inordinate amount of killer hands.

This type of dealer-player partnership is impossible to beat. I can't even tell you how to be on guard for it because it's too difficult to spot. The only way you may get a clue as to what's going on at a table like Bobby's is to realize that you're just losing too many key pots. If you do become aware of losing beyond normal expectations, maybe you should switch tables, which is always a good move—even when you're getting beat repeatedly on the square.

Bobby seemed genuinely elated to have me for his take-off guy. He wanted me to come back to his table the following night, which I did. We cleaned up again. I hung out in Atlantic City a few weeks, stopping in to see Bobby every other day. However, I never returned to see him on subsequent visits to Atlantic City. I guess some kind of defense mechanism preventing me from being part of a scam when I wasn't running it.

Dealer card mechanics

Throughout the poker world you will occasionally spot dealers, if you're trained well enough to do so, who actually still perform the art of dealing seconds. Although this is extremely rare and found only in cardrooms somewhat buffered from strict regulation and mostly outside the English speaking world, you should know that it exists.

Basically what these "mechanics" do is deal a favorable game to their partner or partners at the table. They peek at the top card and hold it back during the hand until it is needed by one of their partners. Good mechanics will combine this talent with other cheating methods such as culling face-up cards from the previous deal and memorizing their order so that the dealer knows everyone's hole cards in the new hand, as Bobby had done with me.

There have also been major poker scams committed by dealers while under the protection of their superiors in public cardrooms. If an expert dealer-mechanic can work with the knowledge that he is beyond scrutiny, you can imagine how terribly effective he would be. I saw one such scam go on at a midsize cardroom in Gardena, California, just a few years ago. It involved not only the dealer and a floorman but the cardroom manager as well. The scam was so blatant that in its openness the victims probably thought nothing of it.

What tuned me into it was that the cardroom manager was actually playing in the game and sitting in Seat 1, immediately to the woman dealer's left. I found it bizarre that he was playing and had thought that public cardroom employees were not permitted to play poker at the establishment employing them. Obviously I was wrong.

Well, if Lady Fingers from *The Cincinnati Kid* was solely a fictitious character, then the real-life Lady Fingers named Cora whom I had in my sights was about the squarest-looking middle-aged black woman I'd ever seen. Yet she was a verifiable card mechanic working a $15–30 seven-stud game. Watching from the rail, I got a bird's-eye view of her peeking at the top card of the deck and occasionally dealing seconds. However, she did not seem to be culling cards to set up the following deals.

I pegged her cohorts as two players at opposite ends of the table, both slick Asians, who would not likely be connected to the frumpy-looking black lady dealer. But cheaters come in all races, shapes and sizes. I must admit that I was quite amused watching their show. The manager, whom I noticed focusing keenly on Cora's movements, was there to protect her. He made friendly conversation with both the Asians he conspired with and the victims at the table, all the while watching out for any threats that might expose their operation.

I observed them work over the game for about 40 minutes until the manager began looking at me suspiciously. Obviously he considered me as a threat to his operation. Little did he know that I was the last person in the world who would rat them out.

Are cheaters using computers to cheat live public poker games?

You've all by now heard about the use of computers in live casinos. They first appeared in the late 1960s to predict where the ball would land on roulette wheels and then later to count cards and make decisions at blackjack. Some of these early inventions were quite successful if not too cumbersome to operate. Later on, we will speak about computers beating computerized poker games online, which does occur very frequently—but has the evolution of computers, lasers and other gadgets reached the brick and mortar poker rooms?

The answer is that they have. In the mid 1980s a regiment of high-tech Silicon Valley geeks developed computers to beat the California cardrooms. The principle was similar to that used with blackjack computers. All face-up cards in the game were entered into the computer, most of the time by pressing down on transmitters in players' shoes, and at the end of hand the computer would make the decision whether to fold, call or raise.

The success of these gizmos, however, was much less remarkable at poker than it was for other casino games. The major fault was that in a high percentage of hands not enough face-up cards were seen. When playing in hold'em games without the collusion of partners signalling their hole cards, you only get to look at a total of seven cards during the entire hand: your two hole cards and the five face-up community cards. And not at the same time. After the deal, all you can enter into the computer is your hole cards. Your pre-flop advantage would be virtually nothing, unless you were receiving information as to what other players in the game were holding in their hands.

After the flop, you can enter three more cards into the computer, which can spit out a calculation to help you decide what you want to do before the turn, and then a sixth card after the turn, which increases your edge going to the river. In some situations the advantage you have on the river, with seven cards (your two and the five on board) entered into the computer, would be more than negligible. However, generally speaking, computerized play in hold'em is not a real winning proposition, unless, of course, you've got some serious collusion going on and you're able to enter several cards into the computer before the flop. I have heard of three and four-man teams playing hold'em with both the computer and collusion, which is indeed a winning parlay.

Omaha offers a better cheating advantage than hold'em if you're playing it with computer help. This is because your own hand contains four cards, twice the amount you'd be able to enter into the computer before the flop (without collusion), and a total of nine cards instead of seven for an entire hand. If you do have partners in the game who can signal you the values of their cards, and you have the time to get them all entered into the computer, which is not always evident, then you certainly have a viable edge on the other players.

In Omaha high–low split games, a collusion team with a computer could really get off, though the operational procedure would be difficult. Imagine if four players in collusion each had a computer console in his sock. It sounds funny, but if they could coordinate the signalling of the hands among one another and the entry of all the cards into their computers, I would think this would be a very dangerous team to contend with.

The best live game to beat would be seven-card stud. In the dealing of this game, you see 57% of the cards for each full hand dealt out to seventh street. Even starting hands that are folded yield 33% to your eyes. So here, even without the collusion, you can enter enough data into your computer for it to make a calculation with much less of a deviation than in the community-card games.

If you've run into a collusion team with a computer in a seven-stud game, you've met an unbeatable situation and can only hope that you'll instinctively know to get up while you still have some bankroll intact.

Another game good for computerized help is lowball or any other five-card draw game. The cards are all dealt face down but you see the five in your hand, which is almost 10% of the deck. This may seem inconsequential but over the long haul you would have a .005% advantage on the deal. Then, depending on how many cards you discard, you will see up to five more (four in standard draw), increasing your mathematical edge. Of course these computers cannot help you decide if the bettor or raiser is bluffing (for that you need your brain), but they can greatly aid in the calculation of card-odds and pot-odds, ultimately telling you whether to call a certain bet or fold the hand.

I would venture to say that with the continuing expansion of online poker, the Silicon Valley geniuses are not bothering much any more with trying to beat cardrooms with computers. They are engaged in their own cat-and-mouse duel against online sites' software and security personnel, and while working their cheating programs online they can't get physically caught with the goods. I doubt that the FBI will come breaking down some online poker player's door with the same intensity they do at residences of hackers spreading viruses to clog up the Internet. So for the time being, at least while online poker rooms remain accessible from the US, don't worry much about running into computer teams at your favorite public poker club.

But still be aware. All the other cheating methods I have described in live poker are very much in proliferation. Pay attention to what is going on around you in the cardroom. Watch out for collusion more than anything else. Card-markers, muckers and other types of card-manipulators are around less but keep an eye open for them as well. While you're not actively involved in a hand, it's a good idea to let your eyes do a little roving. Watch the hands of other people.

They're the two parts of the body from which physical cheating must be launched.

Are bad-beat jackpots kosher?

This is a definite "yes," or as close to one as you can get. Computers would not serve much of a purpose in trying to use collusion to get an aces-full hand burned by four of a kind or a straight flush. The occurrence itself is just too rare and doesn't warrant the time and effort needed to try and bring it about. Computer teams are more interested in working every hand, not the ones that occur only once in several thousand.

If there were a method of cheating which fits jackpot play, it would be card-mucking. If colluding players aiming at the jackpot switched cards, they could conceivably stage the big losing hand required. However, we must not forget that all jackpot hands are very carefully reviewed by surveillance to make sure they are kosher. Therefore, it would be hard to imagine cheaters getting away with fixing up a jackpot in public poker rooms.

On the Internet, however, it can be done. It would take the right program, not only to break down a site's internal software but also to prevent the site from knowing that this has occurred. While I will show you in later chapters how online computer hackers cheat the silicone out of honest players, I doubt that any of them have succeeded in rigging online jackpots.

Cardroom poker cheating outside the United Kingdom. Is it different?

Of course, neither we Americans nor you British hold a monopoly on poker cheating. Europeans and South Americans are just as capable in figuring out ingenious ways of cheating in public poker rooms. It might be true that Americans and

Brits represent the greatest percentage of poker cheats in the world, but they also represent the greatest percentage of honest players.

But what about the types of cheating that go on in French and Dutch brick and mortar cardrooms? Do they vary from what happens in California, Nevada, Atlantic City, Mississippi and London?

Again, it's one of those "yes and no" answers. Cheating in its basic forms are more or less the same on both sides of every ocean. Collusion here works on the same principle as collusion there. No cheater in, say, Madrid, is going to come up with a new way of marking cards unknown in Vegas. By the same token, Vegas's oldest sharpies are not going to come up with marking methods that boggle the minds of the Old Continent's longtime cheaters.

But there are subtle differences between European and American poker cheating. The most important one lies in the first difference you're likely to encounter when stepping foot in Europe: people are speaking foreign languages. This is even true in the United Kingdom. On my last trip to London it seemed that white Anglo-Saxon Protestants actually formed a distinct minority, and when you get inside the once proud city's card clubs it doesn't much change.

So how does the use of multiple languages at the poker table affect cheating? Well, first of all, a lot of players can't understand what a lot of other players are saying. This breeds countless opportunities for players to say things to other players they don't want non-targeted players to understand. Things like "I have ace-king suited" and "Raise me after the flop."

Like in the States, UK poker clubs prohibit the speaking of any language other than English at the tables, but in order to enforce this poker rooms would need bugs installed in the tables—which, by the way, is a common if not standard practice in Great Britain. But still, the people clandestinely listening to the flows and crosscurrents of all that poker-table gibberish would have to be fluent in many languages to weed out the cheat talk from the normal poker chat.

In reality, this English-only rule cannot be strictly enforced. I mean, how many times can a floorperson keep coming over to admonish certain players at the table to "Speak English, please!" You would think such harassment would both tire out and embarrass most floormen charged with that disciplinary function. It would also chase a lot of honest and dishonest foreign-language-speaking players from the games.

Now if the British are going to enforce this Speak English Only edict at UK poker tables, imagine what the French would do! As most of you veterans of European travel know, the French have greater pride in their language and safeguard it more than any other people in the world do theirs. If French players at poker tables in London are subject to "Speak English, please," aren't native anglophones playing poker at the Aviation Club in Paris going to get a huge dose of "Parlez français, s'il vous plaît?" You can bet your *derrière* that the French, who in general terms plainly despise the British, will not put up with the English language on their poker tables if the English are going to reject the language of Molière on theirs.

So all in all, neither country enforces the language rule strictly and therefore many foreign languages prevail at European poker tables.

Another significant difference in European cheating is the increased incorporation of computers and various types of electronic equipment into poker scams. In most European countries, at least as of this writing, computers and electronic gambling paraphernalia are not illegal inside casinos. But if you get caught in an American casino with any gambling device whatsoever, be it computerized or not, you are again faced with an automatic felony charge. With that threat looming over them in US gambling establishments, the high-tech geek-and-freak cheats have taken their operations abroad, where in some European countries there has been a proliferation of computer-based "advantage play."

In Great Britain, where some high-profile cases of computerized casino cheating have stirred the gambling industry, legislation is on the way to outlaw electronic equipment in the casinos. As things on Parliament's agenda are notorious for moving slowly, we can expect it to be some time before gaming devices are forbidden by law to enter UK casinos and card clubs. There are advocates of ridding casinos of gambling devices who say the country's Gaming Act of 1845 might be changed to address this issue as early as 2006.

A third difference pertaining to European cheating is one that has nothing to do with the method utilized but rather with the consequences of getting caught. In American casinos and cardrooms, any attempt of cheating at gambling, no matter what the game or the amount of money in question, is an automatic felony (with the exception of some midwestern states and Indian reservations). This means that if you're caught slipping a dollar chip on a roulette bet after your number won, you are arrested and charged with a felony.

In all of Europe, however, cheaters caught in the act are handled differently: a lot less severe. In Great Britain, for instance, all gambling establishments, whether they're full-fledged casinos or just poker rooms, are private clubs policed by their own security. Brick and mortar casinos in the UK are not permitted to advertise and likewise do not want any negative publicity. Cheating is negative publicity, so instances of it are normally hushed up very efficiently. A prime example of this was the roulette laser scam that beat the London Ritz Club out of $2 million in 2004. Although the scam received widespread publicity when it was uncovered, three other London casinos which fell victim to it kept quiet.

When poker cheats are spotted committing their act in a typical UK cardroom, even if it's as flagrant as marking cards, they are usually rounded up by the internal security staff and hustled off the premises without further incident. Any of those caught cheating who are members of the establishment will automatically have their memberships revoked, and word of the episode will spread to all casinos and cardrooms throughout the UK, whose committees will follow suit with swift revocations. Those cheaters who were merely guests at the card clubs will find it very difficult to reenter UK casinos as *anyone's* guest and face the impossibility of ever becoming a member in their own right.

But this is not nearly as serious as it sounds. The key element is that police are generally not called and no charges are ever pressed against cheaters (with rare exceptions). Whereas in the US players face real prison time when caught cheating, their British counterparts are only subject to getting tossed out the door with a warning not to come back. With the revolving-door entry of guests in UK gambling establishments, those barred find ways to reenter using fake ID and disguise kits.

In Australia, another huge poker territory where the percentage of inhabitants playing the game is greater than anywhere in the world, including the US and the UK, cheaters are subject to prosecution but the penalties are minimal. Someone caught marking cards and bilking players for thousands of Aussie dollars might get a year's probation.

The same basically holds true in Spain, Austria and the Netherlands, three of Europe's most popular poker bastions.

In France, where the game is just as popular, you have to be very impolite when cheating to end up with your ass in the can. In South America, poker cheating is not dealt with very harshly, at least not by the casino authorities. I would be careful, though, about *whom* I cheat down there. I wouldn't want to get caught in Columbia cheating some cartel kingpin. In that case I wouldn't need to worry about what the casino might do to me.

In the Caribbean, where poker is tremendously popular in live casinos, despite the fact that the tropics are home base for many online cardrooms, bosses frown a bit more seriously on cheaters. The casinos are a major part of the islands' tourism industry. Resort operators there don't want people lounging around their pools getting wind of poker scams. There is widespread cheating in Aruba and St Maarten, though I have not heard of anyone actually going to jail on a poker-cheating conviction on either island. However, I have heard about slot-machine crooks rotting in hellhole Aruban prisons.

In the knowledge of lesser criminal penalties to pay on being convicted of gambling crimes, it is not surprising that many cheating teams, including Americans and Brits, favor working the Old Continent's poker rooms. It must be noted, however, that this preference has nothing to do with collusion. Since that form of cheating can hardly be proven, teams practicing it need not worry about what parts of the world punish cheaters more severely than others.

Inasmuch as I've been giving tons of guidance to legitimate players on how to protect themselves against poker cheats, let me give a little advice to you cheaters: best ply your craft in Europe, especially if you're going to cheat with the aid of gadgets, including daub for marking cards. At least if you're unfortunate enough to get bagged over there, you won't have to bear a *Midnight Express* kind of experience.

CHAPTER THREE

THE "UNDERWORLD" SERIES OF POKER

Tournament cheating syndicates

Back in 1994, I attended my first "World Super Bowl of Poker Championships," strictly as a spectator. I had just come off a road trip with my sometime-partners in crime, Preacher and Carla, and Preacher had accumulated a bankroll substantial enough to enter a few events and take several shots at satellites offering a seat for the championship event. I had promised to watch him play but had mixed feelings about whether I wanted him to do well. If he made money during the tournament, he and Carla would be less likely to accompany me on the European casino tour I was planning that summer, and I needed them for my operation.

I watched Preacher blow his entire bankroll at that World Super Bowl of Poker (WSBOP), but during the tournament I unexpectedly observed something much more interesting. In fact, it was phenomenal.

Three different top professional players, who today are the proud owners of multiple WSBOP platinum bracelets, each won two events in a row, and two of the three added a third platinum bracelet to their wrists before the 1994 WSBOP was history. To put these occurrences in their proper perspective, remember that in 1994 the WSBOP comprised but 20 events. So what that means mathematically is that three players won 40% of the events. Care to know the odds of that?

Granted, the fields back then were shorter than the giant ones we see today at the WSBOP, but *three* guys winning two events in a row, and two of the three then tacking on a third win? This was nothing short of incredible, and to me it was *not* credible.

As these probability-defying events unfolded, I decided to take a closer look. One thing you learn while developing into a top international casino cheat is to observe and pick up implicit communication going on around you. In my business, being able to connect people who ostensibly don't know one another and don't want you thinking otherwise is a necessary survival tool. Such skills allowed my escape from the many entrapments casino security personnel laid down for me.

At the point of the tournament where each of these players had locked up two wins, and one a third, I intently watched the next event: $5,000 limit hold'em. All three players were entered.

In the early rounds none of them met at the same table. In the middle rounds two of them were briefly at the same table but both were knocked out. I followed the last of the three throughout the tournament, right down to the final table where he bested the remaining players and won the grand prize, his third victory at the 1994 WSBOP. When I had seen the other two players get eliminated, I considered the possibility that my suspicions were unfounded and almost abandoned my surveillance on the third player.

But something very strange happened before this player made it to the final table. There were three tables remaining in the tournament, two of which had eight players seated, the other seven. The player I focused on was at the table with

seven players, in Seat 3. The size of his chip-stack was somewhere in the middle of the seven stacks on the table. For the
sake of clarity, I'm going to call him "Champ."

On the initial hand that caught my attention, Champ was
under the gun, seated to the left of the big blind. The betting
level of the tournament had reached $4,000–8,000. Before the
flop, he bet $4,000. The next two players in line folded. The
player in sixth position raised, and the player on the button
re-raised. Both blinds folded. Then Champ and the original
raiser called.

The flop came A♦-K♦-J♣. Champ bet $4,000; both sixth po-
sition and the button called. The turn was the 9♣. Champ
made the $8,000 upper-limit bet. Position 6 called, and the
player on the button raised, making it $16,000 and putting
himself all-in. Just after he made that move, I noticed a brief
but marked eye contact between Champ and the guy on the
button. Champ was wearing shades; I couldn't see his eyes,
but I would have have sworn he was glaring at the guy on the
button. He seemed really pissed off about that all-in raise,
more so than just the normal poker reaction when an opponent makes a bet you'd been hoping he wouldn't.

Champ hesitated then cut out the matching chips. Position
6 also called, so the pot remained three-handed going to the
river. The last card the dealer turned was the 3♠, most likely a
blank that helped none of the three remaining hands. Since
the player on the button was all-in, there would be a side pot
between Champ and Position 6, provided there was another
called bet.

Champ did bet the $8,000 but Position 6 promptly folded.
Seeing him do so immediately aroused my suspicions about
the hand. What happened at showdown is probably what
planted the seed in my mind to eventually write this book.

Because the button had gone all-in, a showdown between

Champ and whoever else remained in the pot at the river was imminent. When the dealer called for the hands, Champ flipped over a pair of 7s. Had my suspicions not been heightened, I would have certainly thought that the player on the button had Champ's hand beat. But somehow I was not surprised when the guy showed 10♥-6♥.

The dealer swept the pot to Champ while the player on the button was knocked out of the tournament. Two hands later, the player who'd been in Position 6 lost his remaining chips to Champ, further fueling my suspicions, even though another player lost that pot on the river as well.

I have an excellent memory, which is also a necessity when you cheat casinos for a living. When I reconstructed that hand in my head and analyzed it thoroughly, I came to the conclusion that the three players in that pot were in collusion and that their goal was to pass off all their chips to Champ. By way of that deduction, I came to understand that the reason Champ got so upset when the player on the button raised all-in on the turn was that his raise was a mistake so egregious it exposed their collusion operation.

The other players in the hand who'd folded earlier did not seem to notice what I had, or if they had, offered no outward clues of suspicion. Perhaps they'd been too busy counting their stacks in assessment of where they stood at such a crucial point of the tournament. Very shortly it would condense to two tables, so studying the end of that hand was of less importance.

The mistake the player raising all-in made was to ensure a showdown at the river. When you're involved in collusion, the last thing in the world you want to do is show your hand when you're buck-naked, and when you show 10♥-6♥ to a board of A♦-K♦-J♣-9♣-3♠, you're pretty darn buck-naked.

So what happened in that hand? Let's carefully examine

the play. Before the flop, Champ bets $4,000, is raised by Position 6, who is then re-raised by the button. After the calls, $36,000 (plus the blinds and antes) is in the pot, $24,000 of which came from the eventual losing players. I never saw Position 6's hole cards, therefore, I cannot evaluate the playing of his hand outside the general scheme of things.

But the player on the button is a different story. His starting mid-suited hand at that stage of the tournament is at best a call after an initial raise, even when he's on the button. It's really smarter to fold that hand after a raise. Had he been under the gun and first to act, then a raise may have been the appropriate play, if only in an attempt to steal the pot with two mediocre cards to a straight and a flush. But once there's a raise in front of you, re-raising with those cards becomes a very dangerous move.

After the flop, the player sitting on the button exhibits more suspicious play. No hearts appeared on board, plus he's looking at three strong overcards. So why does he call Champ's $4,000 bet? He sees three potential high pairs against him on board plus he has no flush draw. To make a straight he needs to catch a gut queen, a long shot, and the player in front of him has already called.

Any poker player worth his seat cushion would have to put either Champ or Position 6 on a pair congruent to one of the board cards. It was even possible if not likely that both players paired up on the flop. That much said, you have to conclude that the button called solely to get his money in the pot, as his position-power was completely nullified by his weak hand. If his aim is only to get money into the pot, he must be equally intent on losing the money he puts in the pot, because in no logical way can he expect to draw out and win it.

So now there's $48,000 in the pot, $32,000 of it coming from the eventual losers.

On the turn Champ bets $8,000, and after Position 6 calls, the button raises, putting himself all-in. Absurd! This type of play is not feasible in legitimate high-level tournament play, and here we are at the World Super Bowl of Poker! It doesn't get any higher. What can the guy on the button be thinking? The 9♣ turn card offers him no further possibilities, thus he's drawing dead to a queen on the river. Even if he has the barrel of luck needed to catch it, he could still lose the hand to either a diamond flush or a full house if the board pairs.

So again, why did the button raise all-in? The answer is the same: he wanted to get all his chips into the pot, and he wanted to lose all his chips to Champ. But then, if my reasoning is right on, why would the button make this move knowing his weak hand would be exposed at showdown? Surely, he (they) could have waited for a hand offering some camouflage under which he could have passed off his chips without being so blatantly obvious.

Here I have to take painstaking pause and then finally resume by saying that the player on the button simply screwed up. Let's remember that there is a lot of money at stake in these WSBOP tournaments, and the key to success for cheaters in collusion is to pass off chips at the most opportune moments. The pressure of correctly carrying out these moves can certainly derail the concentration of the people involved in them. I know this firsthand. There is tremendous pressure in organized casino cheating, whether it is at the blackjack table or at the poker table.

The player on the button most likely suffered a mental lapse whereon he simply forgot that his hand would be naked at showdown. That's why Champ appeared so annoyed and somewhat in disbelief, because through signalling he knew that his cohort on the button had nothing and that at showdown everyone would know it as well. The revelation of their hands would certainly tickle a couple of funny bones. Had any chips remained in front of the button-player after he raised, Champ surely would have signalled him not to bet any more and fold his hand on the river.

So now the pot has been doubled to $96,000, of which $64,000 has been contributed by the eventual losers. The river card comes and Champ bets $8,000 at the remaining player in Position 6. That player promptly folds. It's true that at this point he still has chips in front of him, but he cannot commit the same faux pas inadvertently made by the button on the turn. If he does not have the goods in his hand, he's got to fold; the team can't have *two* naked hands at showdown.

So, despite the gaffe, Champ's stack is enriched by $64,000, and he goes on to the final table with good ammunition. Both players who lost that pot are out of the tournament and now watching Champ from the rail. Neither seems to be even the least bit upset about having been eliminated. Does this seem strange? Does it seem stranger when I tell you that over the next three years of watching Champs A, B and C (Champs B and C being the other two multiple-winners at the 1994 WSBOP) perform at the WSBOP, the same two guys who lost that questionable pot to Champ A in 1994 also lost big pots to all three champs as the tournaments winded down toward final tables? Naturally these two guys were eliminated early in some of the tournaments, as were the champs, but I observed a distinct pattern of play and outcomes about which I am absolutely certain.

Three years after that, I witnessed two of the three champs have another tremendous run at the WSBOP, and the same "losing" players were often involved in key pots with the champs, who continually raked in their chips. In fact, I never saw one of these losers beat any of the champs for a pot. And they never seemed pissed off about it.

The bottom line of my now 10 years of "scrutinizing" the World Super Bowl of Poker is that something shifty is definitely going on. Which brings us to a very big question.

Does cheating take place at the world's major poker tournaments?

Well, I'm going to let you answer this question, without serving up a stupid prompt like "Is the pope Catholic?" First of all, let's take any major tournament and examine it. Got any ideas which one we should choose? Let's make it simple. We've already revisited a hand from the 1994 World Super Bowl of Poker, so why not leave there and take a look at the WSOP? Yes, the one and only World Series of Poker that any sane poker player or observer would have to nod his head when it was suggested that this is the grandest poker tournament of them all, the one that poker dreams are made of.

The first thing we're going to do is take a look at its players. But before we do, I must stress that in no way, shape or form am I trying to single out any well-known professional poker players. In fact, to protect myself as well as them, I am going to refer to all the poker players I cite in examples by using simple letters preceded by "Player." We will again have Player A, Player B, Player C and so on. In this fashion nobody can sue me, or if in the strange case a famous poker player wants to brag to his buddies that I'm talking about him or her, he or she cannot prove I'm talking about him or her.

Here are questions to consider on the path leading to the answer to the big question whether cheating goes on in major tournaments. When reading ahead, keep in mind that all the data I present concerning the World Series of Poker is consistent with research I have done into *all* major tournaments. I am saying that the patterns I have identified at the WSOP are as easily identifiable at all the World Poker Tour events and all the independent major tournaments in California, Mississippi, Connecticut, Atlantic City and Europe.

Scenario 1

Question: What is the difference in the actual level of skill among top poker players willing to cough up thousands of dollars to play in the WSOP's 41 events (as of this writing) and 10 grand for the championship?

Answer: Not much. I'd say 1 or 2%. Others trying to discredit my theory might say two or three.

Analysis: That's right. There is actually very little difference in skill levels between the players who write the books and the ones who read them. If a certain level of experience is attained, in terms of time spent or hands played, there is no one in the world more than 2% better than anyone else in the world, given that no one in the statistical sample is retarded, autistic or suffering from a mental ailment capable of impairing poker sense. This means that the distribution of players reaching the final table and winning tournaments should not deviate from the range of random outcome by more than 2% over the long run.

If you create any hypothetical poker situation for the world's top hundred players, then ask each what his course of action would be given a set of game conditions and circumstances, they would reliably offer up very similar strategies, more or less play the hand the same way.

Just look at the books written by today's top pros. They have extensively treated every poker game and poker situation under the sun. They give strategies for live ring games, tournaments and online play. In explaining their methods of winning poker, these authors all paint numerous detailed examples of how to play certain hands within the constraints of bankroll, table position and other characteristics of the game needed to accurately assess the situation. If you read a large number of these books, you will notice how their theories don't vary much. They are all experts on the game. When you get to their level of play, you've reached a plateau from which you cannot ascend higher. It's a situation comparable to chess. All the grandmasters know the moves inside and out. The difference in skill-level between Bobby Fischer and Gary Kasporov is certainly less than 2%.

In the 2005 WSOP there were more than 5,600 players in the championship event. And if you add those who played in other events but not the championship, you've got hundreds more. Now, the majority of these players never see the final table in the big event, regardless of how many times they enter it. But this can be expected because there is only one final table and only nine players can make it there. Comparatively speaking, you've got to hit a pretty decent-size trifecta of long-shot horses to be one of the lucky ones.

I did some research into the experience-levels of the 2005 WSOP field of players. I found that a great percentage of them had at least five years' poker tournament experience, either online or in live events. I've spoken to many who have told me that any proficient player can win a big tournament on any given day. The overriding cause of that randomness is due to tournaments' betting structures. As they increase on every round, a player must constantly win key hands to advance. To do that you must be lucky.

Some players have confided in me that they don't like tournaments because there is too much luck involved. If there really is too much luck involved, it would seem to me that repetitive wins in major tournaments would occur less than if skill alone were the predominant factor. I mean, how many times can luck dominate? True, I've heard many a poker play say "I'd rather be lucky than good," but another favorite say-ing among pro players is that the "cream always rises to the top." So which of these is true?

Scenario 2

Question: Since the late 1980s, has the distribution of players reaching WSOP final tables and winning events been consis-tent with entry fields of players no more than 2% better or worse than anyone else in these fields? (I'm starting in the late 1980s because in previous years fields were too small for accurate statistical analysis)

Answer: Hardly.

Analysis: In every year the WSOP has been held since 1989, you can throw these statistical deviation charts out the window. If you go back and look at the results for the last 15 years, your mind should become boggled by the amount of "luck" certain players have had.

Back in the early and mid 1990s, when the number of events did not yet break the 30-barrier, a handful of famous players had constant staggering results. Imagine *winning* three events out of 15 you played in when the averaged true odds (let's even say they're adjusted in your favor because you're the best tournament player in the world) are at least 100 to 1 for each event. How lucky can you get? The chances of a 100-to-1 shot coming in three times out of 15 simply can-not happen at the WSOP.

The main reason why is that those odds are really skewed higher than that. That's because the blinds and antes are al-ways increasing. And when you lose a big hand in the later stages of a tournament, you're usually all-in and knocked out. In order to get to the final table, you have to survive the blows hammering away at you relentlessly from every corner of each preceding table, and then to win the tournament you have to survive it all over again. Sound difficult? It's damned impossible! Yet select players several times have displayed this required luck and won multiple events at the WSOP.

Scenario 3

Question: Is it only winners of tournaments who've displayed this incredible luck? Or are other players reaching final tables with a frequency defying the odds?

Answer: Lo and behold, there is a certain number of players who have been so lucky to reach the final table so many times you would think they sneaked into tournaments when only two tables remained, and got away with it the way a cyclist would sneak into the pack a mile away from the finish line and beat Lance Armstrong to win the Tour de France.

Analysis: Go back and review the WSOP results for the last 15 years. This time pay attention to those who made the final table in smaller and average-size events. Widen your scope to the two final tables in the larger events. Don't worry about doing an analysis on "cashing." Except for the large tournaments, most of the players finishing in the money are not taking much in addition to their entry fee to the bank. Although the distribution of prize money has recently become more lucrative for those on the lower rungs of the cash ladder, it does not alter what I'm trying to show you here.

You will see that each distinctive time period (say three or four years) reveals a certain set of players who had an uncanny ability to reach the final tables.

Scenario 4

Question: Did you ever wonder about all this "chopping" that goes on when two, three or four players are left at the final table?

Answer: You should.

Analysis: If anything reeks—I mean really stinks of collusion!—this is it. It happens at almost every final table. One guy is sitting there with more than half the chips, but he's feeling generous enough to split the first and second-place prize money with the player in position to become runner up. I've even seen guys with three-quarters of the chips or more display the magnanimous behavior to split the prize money with runner-ups whose stacks looked like totem poles next to the chip-leaders' fortresses of chips resembling the United Nations Building.

I've always found this practice to be suspicious, albeit it's the only outward example of the WSOP collusion I'm about to attest to. Perhaps this is kind of a reverse psychology used by those big-time poker players looking to conceal the real deal-making taking place *before* the tournament even started.

Scenario 5

Question: What about tournament players buying shares in each other before the start of the tournament?

Answer: More than two-thirds of the players who reach the final table at the WSOP championship own only a fraction of themselves. This means that they have sold off investment shares to other poker players who may or may not be competing against them in the very same tournament. An example of this: Player A needs $10,000 to enter the championship event. He only has $2,500. Now he needs to raise an additional $7,500 to obtain his seat. He does this by selling off shares of himself. Player B invests $5,000 in Player A and Player C invests $2,500. The result of this poker "venture" is that Player A owns 25% of himself while Player B and Player C own 50% and 25%, respectively. Players B and C's investments are not loans, therefore, should Player A bust out of the tournament, Players B and C are out their money. On the other hand, should Player A finish in the money, Players B and C receive 50% and 25% of the cash paid out to Player A.

This is all common business practice, no different than three persons investing in a delicatessen. But what raises eyebrows with this poker tournament scenario is seeing Players B and C competing in the same tournament as Player A, whom they invested in. On the surface it would seem like this situation brings about a conflict of interests. What happens if all three of these players make it deep down into the tournament, say the final 10 tables? Players B and C would be playing against their own money when opposing Player A in a pot. So how do they approach this?

You guessed it. The ominous poker demon comes into play: collusion. Players A, B and C must play as a team in order to maximize the profits to be split among its three members. This is why there have been so many public accusations of softplaying and chip-dumping shrouding the WSOP.

Analysis: This phenomenon seeing players investing in other players whom they play against will always be present at major poker tournaments. When you have entry fees as steep as $10,000, even $25,000, there will always be players looking to "piece themselves off," for it's the only way they can get a seat in the tournament. In some instances, the investors, say Players B and C from the previous example, may not even inform their horse, Player A, that they will be working a collusion scam should either Player B and/or Player C end up at the same table as Player A.

In certain tournaments, one high-rolling player-investor might have a piece of as many as 50 players. So you can imagine how prevalent the collusion would become. In fact, it becomes a necessity, and more than that a very fine-tuned apparatus for taking down bundles of cash at the WSOP. The cover that the syndicates afford themselves while making these murky deals is the simple fact that they don't appear to be hiding anything. Now I am going to repeat the original question, or at least rephrase it:

In view of the facts that the percentage difference of skill between top professional tournament players is no more than 2%, and that the deviation of this distribution for those reaching the final table is more like 20%, and that the chopping up of tournament prizes goes on more than that of beef, chicken and shrimp at Benihana restaurants, do you think there is some collusion going on at the WSOP?

This time I am not going to answer for you. I will only show you how it's done.

First, let's review the definitions of card-odds and pot-odds. Card-odds are the odds against you making the winning hand you're drawing to. Pot-odds determine if the money already in the pot warrants you to put additional money in the pot to buy the chance of drawing. If the pot-odds are not greater than the card-odds, then you don't want to put your money in. You fold your hand.

Same thing works for the totality of a major tournament. Remember, though, that there is one major difference between the WSOP and the British Open golf tournament. That is when entering the WSOP you have to pay your entry fee. If someone else sponsors you, they get a percentage of the money you win. At the British Open, the entrants do not have to put up any money, therefore, no financial risk to them is involved. If they don't cash then maybe they go home hungry, but they didn't lose $10,000.

For a professional tournament player, the decision to enter the WSOP is based on crucial criteria. About the most crucial is: Is it worth it? In other words, does the money-odds exceed the pot-odds, which in this case are the costs of playing in the tournament.

At the WSOP championship, 5,600 players put up $10,000 apiece. That creates a total prize-money pool of more than $50 million. The way the prize money is structured, from $7.5 million for the winner down to 12 grand for finishing 500th, a player certainly doesn't have pot-odds in his favor going in. If you looked solely at first place, you might consider the following determination: If the odds are roughly 5,600 to 1 against you winning and you paid $10,000 to enter, then your first prize should you win needs to be how much to be worth it?

Well, if it were a winner-take-all freeze-out then the answer would be anything more than $56 million. But if that were the case, I doubt anyone would play the championship. The WSOP would more resemble a huge state's lottery than a poker tournament. So we must take for granted that the top 200 finishers should be paid prize money in order to maintain an interesting an exciting tournament. But there is a problem that disturbs the financial symmetry of the tournament: mainly the money the host casinos remove from the entry fees to pay expenses and take commissions. Which means there's less money going out than has been put in. It's kind of like a slot machine.

So why then do the professional players play? If the money-odds aren't right, is it solely to satisfy their egos? I have a definite opinion on this. My poker-playing partners Preacher and Carla both have gargantuan egos. Many other poker players I have come to know over the years also have oversized egos. But 5,600 of them? You can't tell me that players smart enough to be among the cherished poker elite of the world are dumb enough to shell out that kind of entry money only to indulge their egos. I highly doubt it.

The truth is that they would never muster up that kind of cash for such a shallow reason. But they do show up in record-breaking numbers, don't they? I'm going to tell you why, but first let's examine why lesser skilled players are also coming to the WSOP in increasing droves.

Many players arriving in Las Vegas amid all the hoopla of the tournament do so only to rub shoulders with the best, and then try to become the best while rubbing. These players can and often do get lucky. We've seen several unknowns walk away with the championship in the past 10 years, which proves luck has its place in the WSOP.

In recent years we have also witnessed the presence of a growing bunch of celebrities who chalk up the $10,000 entry-fee-loss as publicity for their next release, whether it be a book, movie or song. We've all heard about the poker-playing exploits of Ben Affleck. Perhaps he is a terrific poker player. After all, he did take down a $300,000 first prize at a California poker tournament. But, come on, the vast majority of the poker-smitten celebrities, with the possible exception of a former Russian tennis player who's won both the French and Australian Opens, has no business banging heads with the real poker pros we see on TV more often than the TV stars who moonlight playing tournament poker.

Next there are the pure dreamers and the whim-actors, otherwise put, those who act on a whim. Ever hear of fantasy baseball camps? That's where any old schmo who was a failure in Little League can make up for it by spending a summer weekend with real former major leaguers. Who would have ever in their wildest dreams believed that one day there would exist poker boot camps? Well, they do, and people fork up thousands to spend a weekend in a Vegas hotel really learning how to play like the pros, who serve as their poker drill sergeants.

These people presently account for a significant percentage of entrants to the World Series. When I think about it, I relish the idea of opening my own boot camp for aspiring casino cheaters who always dreamed about ripping off casinos but never had my balls. I bet I'd get some campers, although their numbers would undoubtedly not rival those the poker pros get.

Now let's get back to the real pros and why they come to the WSOP. If I've already explained that the money-odds don't make it worth their while, what does? You guessed it: the money-odds. No, it's not a printing error. What the wise-guys on the poker circuit do is *make* it worth their while, and the only way to do that is to bring the money-odds high enough to justify the entrance fees. Are we starting to connect now?

It's called the WSOP Consortium and it's as organized as any Fortune 500 company. To show you how it works, I will return to my roster of professional poker players and select six of them: Player A, Player B, Player C, Player D, Player E and Player F. These players know each other very well and don't have to hide that fact from anyone at the WSOP. Their record of successful tournament play and revered places on the all-time WSOP cash-earnings list hoist them above scrutiny. But, as I will show you, they're not such unbelievably great tournament players in their own individual rights, and they're not as honest as most poker authors would have you believe. But when working together they are one hell of a for-midable force.

The six players have a nice dinner together the night be-fore the tournament opens. Most likely it takes place in Bin-ion's steakhouse, where I myself had dinner while being in-terviewed by *Maxim* magazine. Over their juicy steaks and Idaho potatoes they discuss strategy, but only minimally be-cause they already know it so well.

Back in one of their suites, they count up their combined bankroll. Say it's $300,000. Each player staking 50 grand to the bank for this type of major tournament is reasonable. If they go bad, all these guys have enough cash to refill their collective tank.

Tomorrow's opening event is limit hold'em. The entry fee is $1,500. The consortium invests $9,000 to get all their horses in the starting gate. First prize tops $300,000. Each finisher at the final table is handsomely paid. It is determined that Player A, Player B and Player C are to be the go-to players, called the "receivers." This means that Player D, Player E and Player F want to get their chips to them at some opportune moment in the tournament, usually when limits are about to be raised and tables are condensed. The three players assigned to pass off their chips to the receivers are called "suppliers."

The consortium desires that each of its six players draw seats at different tables at the start of the event. In the early stages of tournament play, this would be optimal from a logistics point of view. Each player would then have the opportunity on his own to accumulate as many chips as he could. But if two players find each other at the same opening table, it is not a serious problem. They would just have to softplay around each other while being aggressive against the other players' stacks. At any time, roles among team members may be switched. Even though Players A, B and C have been designated as receivers, the three remaining players are able to fill that role should it become necessary.

As people inevitably get knocked out of the tournament and the number of tables shrink, members of the consortium are bound to end up at the same table, provided, of course, they're still alive in the tournament. So after a few hours of play, Player A and Player D find themselves at the same table. They play their best tournament poker in the hope that each of them can accumulate chips, and each takes special care not to knock the other out of the tournament. Play continues in this mode as they get deeper into the tournament. The same basic collusion techniques I've previously described in ring games also play a role, but they need to be finer tuned. A player raising only to build a bigger pot for his partner to win loses his chips in the process; he cannot rebuy (unless it's a rebuy tournament). With that limitation, there can be no screw-ups.

At a key time in the tournament, usually when the field has dwindled down to where everyone remaining is within two tables of reaching the final table, the big collusive moves are made. They involve dumping chips.

If Player A and Player D remain on the same table and each has about the same number of chips, it may be possible that neither has enough chips to make a sustained go of it at the next consolidated table. However, if one or the other had all their chips, he would be much better armed to go at it alone. Thus often the sacrifice of a supplier to pump up a receiver with chips is the preferred strategy of tournament cheating consortiums. In fewer cases, the two keep their stacks and advance to the next table. Each situation is different and is discussed among the players during breaks in play, or right at the table using predetermined signals when urgent.

The dump takes place when the supplier purposely loses a pot to the receiver. The values of the hands are not very important. Deep in tournament play, weak hands often get the money, so it would be hard to accuse someone of being in a pot at the river for any other reason than trying to win it.

After evaluating the situation and determining the right moment, either the supplier or receiver makes a heavy raise over the big blind. This is designed to get other players out of the pot. At this stage in the tournament, small-handed pots frequently take place, so a big pre-flop raise more than not gets the job done. The ideal situation for chip-dumping is to have the players in collusion going at it heads-up, but that's not always possible.

If one of the other players calls, a dangerous situation can develop where the supplier ends up supplying the wrong player with chips. However, if the moment for the coup has been well chosen, this rarely happens. Then with the supplier and receiver heads-up, they go through the motions of playing the hand with enough bets and raises to get the supplier all-in. Then at showdown they hope the receiver's hand prevails. It usually does because part of determining the right moment to dump off chips had entailed signalling each other the value of their hole cards.

In the event that this scheme backfires and the supplier wins the hand, another attempt at the chip-dump must be made as soon as possible. If that fails as well and the receiver gets busted out of the tournament, then the supplier, now with all their chips, is forced to move onward to the next table, where he may continue in his newfound function as a receiver or revert back to being a supplier, depending on many variables such as how many of the consortium's players remain in the tournament and the amount of their chip-stacks.

And so the consortium moves onward to the final table. Naturally it won't make it there every time, but if its six players are as fundamentally sound as the other 7,000 competing at the World Series, they certainly will have created positive-return situations by making the pot-odds of the tournament greater than what they should be based on entry fees and standard distribution of prize money. Each time the consortium gets one of its players to a final table, a very healthy profit for that event is realized.

As most of you know, 41 events were staged at the 2005

WSOP. Collusion among top tournament players is effective in all of them, but certain events lend the greatest opportunities for helping a partner along on his road to the final table. One form of poker that is especially conducive to collusion by professional tournament players is Omaha high–low split (or Omaha 8-or better). Its first attractive element is simply that it's a split-pot game. Two players split the pot provided someone has an 8 low or better. Therefore, at a full table with nine or 10 players, you have players chasing high hands, others chasing low hands, and still others chasing both. This wide spectrum of possibilities leads to many wild pots, and most of the time a higher average number of players will stay in them to see the turn and river cards.

When professional players work a tournament split-pot game they have many advantages. First and foremost is that they are actually playing four hands (given a two-man team at the table) against the rest of the table. This is because each player has a chance to capture the nut high and the nut low. If one of the desired outcomes is realized, then they can implement a relentless raise and re-raise assault against all those players chasing the opposite winning hand.

Imagine how strong that is when the nuts appear on the flop. This happens often enough with low hands. If Player A flops a wheel (a perfect low of A-2-3-4-5), he at that point has made the nut low hand, and, barring a flush, the nut high one. But just having the nut low is enough firepower to get the raising-re-raising barrage going. The only way to get hurt is if someone else at the table also makes the nut low and you end up splitting half the pot ("getting quartered"). In most practical circumstances, this does not happen enough to offset the profit amassed by gearing up the artillery once you have the wheel. I have, however, seen cheating teams screw themselves by whipsawing with the best low hand on the flop, only to get it counterfeited by a better low hand made on the turn or river. Experienced teams won't often trap themselves like that.

To make this underhanded style of play even more alluring at Omaha high–low, the players colluding are given cover that is not afforded them in traditional pot games.

Let's resume the aforementioned example. Player A has made the nut low on the flop. His hole cards are A-5-10-K. The flop came 4-3-2, so he's got his wheel. Player B, on the other end of the table, has 10-J-Q-Q. After the flop he's still got a high pair, and let's say a flush draw as well. Knowing that his partner has the wheel, Player B will raise the pot each time the action comes to him, unless he deems that too much raising will scare away other players pursuing high hands. However, in most high–low pots, there is someone bent on making a high hand, mainly because in many pots there won't be a qualifying low to split with.

Let's assume that a third "honest"and amateur player in the game has A-4-4-7 and flopped an ace-high flush draw to go with his set of 4s. Plus he's got a wheel draw to a 5. Even though skilled players would probably fold this hand because it's currently losing both high and low to a possible wheel, our weaker player is seduced by its possibilities. He's already got trips and has a 1 in 3 chance of making both a flush and a full house, either of which would virtually lock him to the winning high hand. Therefore, when Player B bets and Player A raises, that third player trapped between them will not only call the bet and raise but will call again when Player B re-raises, and then again when Player A caps.

Player B's actions would be foolish had he been playing on the up and up. His hand of 10-J-Q-Q, even with the overpair and flush draw, is not that strong. But the important twist is that his hand is good enough to avoid suspicious light on his re-raise. Some players do like to raise, even re-raise, on the "come" as long as they have feasible possibilities to draw out. In Player B's case, a queen on the turn or river would give him trips and possibly the winning high hand, especially if the board paired and he made a full house with queens. The appearance of chasing those possibilities gives Player B credibility for his actions.

With all that action, the worst the partnership could do is end up splitting the pot. In any given case that could spell a loss of money, but in the long run hands played out in this fashion will make combined tournament stacks grow, and in side games make bankrolls fatten. This is because you very often have four or five players chasing the pot to the river, and they're getting cut up pretty good along the way.

So now you see why split-pot games are so good to cheaters. But you're asking yourself aloud, "How the hell do they signal their partners the values of their hands?" There are just so many possibilities.

It's not so complicated. As you might suspect, since the game is high–low, cheaters will use the high part of the card to signal high hands and the lower portion of it to signal low hands. Suited high cards are indicated by two chips neatly placed on the same card positions I've outlined for hold'em. That configuration covers all high-running straight and flush draws. For high pairs only one chip on the corresponding spots is used. Pairs lower than 10s are not signalled, because unless there is a wheel draw on the low side to go with them, they don't qualify as a playable hand.

Let's go back to Player A's hand. He has no pair, no flush draw, but does have two key low cards. How does he signal? He lays his four cards neatly down and places one chip at the bottom of the pile in the middle.

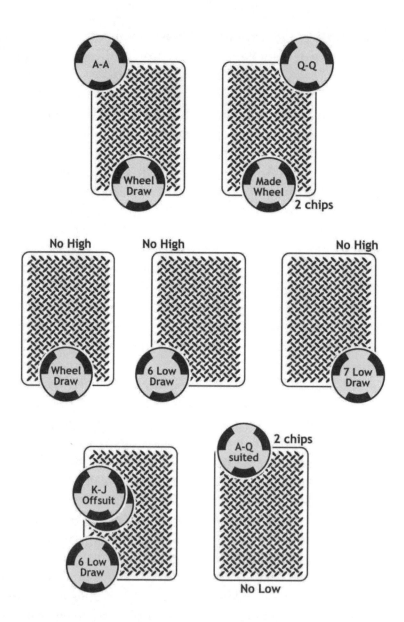

This means he is drawing to a wheel. Since in Omaha you can only use two of your four cards together with the com-

munity cards to make a hand, it doesn't matter if you have
three or four cards to the wheel. You can use *only* two, therefore, you signal that you are drawing to a wheel. Your two
cards are somewhere between A and 5; you need not specify.
If you make the wheel on the flop, as did Player A, you drop
a second chip atop. Once your cohort sees the signal, you pull
the chips off.

If you start with two cards drawing to a 6 low, you place
that original single chip on the bottom left side of the pile. If
it's a 7 low you're drawing to, you place it on the bottom
right. Drawing to an 8 low without a good high hand is not
playable, therefore, no signal is given for the 8.

What if you have a high pair and two cards to the wheel?
How would you signal both without giving the appearance
you're playing "connect the dots" with chips spread all over
your cards? Well, cheaters working collusion angles have two
schools of thought on this. One is to use the card high and
low at the same time, meaning that if you have a pair of aces
and a wheel draw, you put one chip on the top left corner of
the card and another on the bottom-middle of the card. Is this
too obvious? Not if the hustlers are skilled enough to create
distractions and illusions. These acts may be likened to a
baseball third-base coach flashing signals to his batter. Have
you ever noticed all the arm-flailing and brushing these
coaches do? All those fingers-to-their-shoulders-and-elbows
routines? Well, somewhere in all that is the actual signal
whether to hit or take a pitch, steal a base, hit and run, or
whatever options are available for that given play.

It works the same for signalling hands at the poker table. If
a good chip-handler is constantly playing with his chips:
shuffling them, cutting and stacking them, and so on, he can
for a second drop the necessary chips on his cards and then
remove them to get back into his act. It's really quite easy. I

can tell you that much from my own experiences. When I worked the collusion gig with Preacher and Carla in Aruba, I became very deft at chip choreography—to the point that in between all that juggling, I could slide the chip-signals onto the cards and then slip them off with the coolness of a ballerina. And I have to admit that both Preacher and Carla were even better than I.

The second school of thought on high–low communication is to use only half of the card, preferably the bottom.

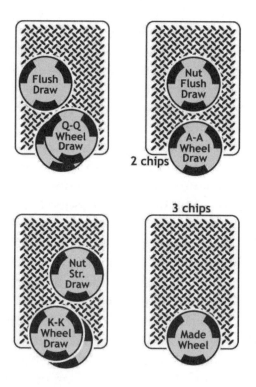

The same pair of aces with a wheel draw can be portrayed by neatly placing two chips at the bottom-middle of the card. The chip underneath represents your wheel draw, the chip above your pair of aces. Then if you make your wheel, you drop another chip on it. If you have a pair of kings with the wheel draw, you slant the second chip slightly to the left. If it's queens, slant it slightly to the right; jacks, slant it slightly upward and 10s slightly behind. If your starting hand is a wheel and flush draw, you still flash your wheel draw with the single chip at bottom-middle. Then you lay a second chip at the center of the card if you have the nut flush draw. If it's not the nut flush draw, you place that chip at left-center. A single chip at right-center would indicate the nut straight draw.

I know this sounds a little overwhelming to a lot of you, but it really is super functional. My purpose is not to make expert card-signallers out of you but only to show you how it's done. If you want to take a closer look at these chip-signalling configurations, take out a deck of cards and a box of poker chips and do it yourself. Just follow the patterns I've outlined and diagrammed and you'll see how simple and efficient it is. The facet of it that requires some practice is to make your chip placements and removals seem nothing more than part of the continuous flow of playing with your stacks. It should also be noted that in high–low games not every single playable hand is signalled among colluders; trying to do so would be overwhelmingly difficult. But, I assure you, the percentage of hands that is relayed by cheaters makes collusion in split-pot games quite appetizing.

Another thing I should mention: some lowball cheaters don't even bother with signals. The game is so wide open you don't even need to use your chips. If one cheater's partner is positioned close enough on the table, he simply flashes the cohort his hand. The flashing motions are quick so that only players intended to see the cards notice.

In low games that use a wild card, collusion teams can

really put the hurt on honest players, especially in the California ring games. In five-card-draw lowball with a joker, I have seen people play spectacularly bad, especially when holding the joker before the draw. It seems to me that scores of California lowball players believe they cannot lose if the joker comes to them off the deal.

There's no question that lowball players, even the bad ones, are a breed apart. They're devious by nature. They make steely bluffs like raising before the draw and then standing pat, making you ponder the probability that they're sitting with a made 6 or 7 low. Then you call them down and are flabbergasted when they're sitting there with a self-crippling two pair. Then the very next hand they'll do the same thing. And, by golly, this time they got the wheel.

So imagine the golden, or I should say platinum opportunities offering themselves like naked women to lowball collusion teams. Even the signalling is easier because you're picking up five cards, and some players fan them out ever so slowly to get more juice out of the peek. By going through the same motions, cheaters can emit information. They can use the table surface without the cards for their signals.

I am not going to give you any more primers on signalling. It's just too doggone easy. But when you're dealt the joker with A-2-3-K in your hand, and your partner has 2-3-4-5-Q, and some poor guy scrunched between you with a lot of chips raises, be prepared to open fire with everything you've got. I mean in lowball *even* cheaters have to gamble a little. True, neither one of you has a pat low, but there's a heck of a good chance one of you will make out okay on the draw.

Now let's finally get back to the WSOP. In all 40 events leading up to the big daddy of 'em all, the $10,000 no-limit hold'em championship, cheating by collusion has taken place. Trust me, it's the truth. I have seen it repeatedly and I am not someone who mistakes cheating for luck or for skill.

But what about this grand championship? Do professional tournament cheating syndicates dare cheat at the greatest event in the history of the poker world? One that now has more followers than NASCAR. Or do they show some measure of respect to the true poker legends who both play in this lofty event and watch over it from majestic picture frames on the Horseshoe's deified walls?

Respect? Are you kidding? Get outta here! There's more than $50 million involved. You want money or you want respect? Besides, those guys staring out from the walls are mostly dead or has-beens, anyway. Do I sound irreverent? Maybe so, but I'm only telling you the truth.

Do pride and ego come into play? Would either one prevent a poker player who cheats from cheating? Is it possible that just one time even the most hardcore cheater would resort to venerable means to try and win the WSOP championship? All by himself? Perhaps to satisfy his ego? Or to take pride in such an accomplishment, to be able to look at himself in the mirror and say, "I won the World Series of Poker and I did it honestly!"

If we're really going to delve into the minds of cheaters, we must first understand why professionals cheat.

We will examine that question later.

Other forms of cheating at the WSOP

Besides collusion, are there other forms of cheating prevalent at the WSOP? I would have to say that if the answer were yes, it would be rare.

But the answer is still yes.

Blatant forms of cheating, such as mucking and switching cards, would require not only tremendous balls but also a lot of stupidity to go with them. The WSOP is scrutinized more than any other event in professional poker. It is strictly presided over by its tournament officials, who run a very tight ship. In addition, undercover Nevada Gaming Control Enforcement agents patrol the premises. Then you have the observation of TV commentators and millions of people getting a look at it on television, not to mention the players and spectators present at the tables. So to try any cheating moves in front of countless roving eyes and surveillance and TV cameras would be tantamount to trying to slip naked into a church choir unseen.

There is, however, one form of cheating that might be attempted at the WSOP, though I cannot say I have seen it go down. That would be marking cards with a disappearing solution. But again, such an undertaking would be extremely bold, and to do this at a final table suicidal because someone would have to notice you going to your solution. It would be no different than a spitball pitcher in the seventh game of the baseball World Series going to the gel in his waistband on national TV.

So all in all, if you've never played the WSOP before, or have but are nevertheless leery about its integrity, you need only be aware of collusion. It's a pretty safe bet you won't run into anything else going on beneath the table. But there is, however, one little dishonest thing that has recently come to light.

Tournament chip cheating

Now here's a form of cheating that takes place in major tournaments, including the WSOP, and requires big balls. Over the years, there have been chip-counterfeiting operations in casinos everywhere. They were all aimed against the main cashiers of casinos, where fake chips could be passed off as real ones and then exchanged for cash. In order to get away with these fraudulent transactions, chip counterfeiters had to produce an excellent product able to pass muster under the wary eyes of scrutinizing tellers at the casino cage. Many of these scams ran smoothly for admirable lengths of time, but eventually they all got busted for going to the well one time too many.

At the 2005 World Series of Poker, we saw a variation of this. It was a lot more subtle and claimed to have been an accident, but after I tell you how these scams can greatly abet their instigators, you can make your own judgment about what happened there.

What took place at the Rio Hotel-Casino during the $2,000 no-limit hold'em event may not have been the tip of an iceberg but it was certainly a drip from an icicle. Two black souvenir poker chips that are nearly indistinguishable when stacked with actual $100 tournament chips being used in the WSOP were discovered in play. These chips are on sale in the gift shop right outside the Rio's poker hall where the tournament was staged. They are emblazoned with the WSOP logo in the center, which differs from the real tournament chips that have "100" stamped in the middle. But on their side-edges, both series of chips contain similar alternating black-and-white speckling.

Naturally tournament organizers were concerned that a new form of tournament cheating had crept up and bitten them. One of the tournament supervisors was immediately alerted to the existence of the first of the phony chips. His response was to take the chip out of play and replace it with a regulation chip, without penalizing the player, who undoubtedly was shitting a brick. The supervisor stated in all honesty that tournament officials didn't know if the player caught with the chip had brought it into the tournament or if it was part of the set-up chips officials had laid out for him at the start of the event, which (unstated by the supervisor) would have meant the bogus chip had been entered into a previous event by someone using it by design.

If that weren't bad enough for the WSOP's image, a second phony $100 chip was discovered in play at another table. The supervisor at that table made the same decision: replace it with a regulation chip. At the end of play, the assistant tournament director announced that from that point on, players holding phony chips would have them confiscated without their being replaced, and that anyone caught purposely slipping fakes into play (although hard to prove) would be immediately disqualified without being able to recover his buy-in money. He further said that WSOP dealers and surveillance personnel had been told to be on guard against phony chips entering play.

In discussions overheard throughout that day, tournament bigwigs were repeatedly assuring everyone, including ESPN writers who were anxious to run with the fodder, that the embarrassing discovery of two phony chips was an isolated instance no doubt the result of a simple accident. One of the theories pawned off to eager listeners was that players were using these phony chips to cover their hole cards, the way they often do with cigarette lighters and good luck charms. Another was that they simply were what they were: souvenirs. But I know better and am obligated to tell you what's going on.

I'm going to introduce you to a new term I coined myself: "chip-doping." If it reminds you of sports-doping, it's supposed to.

It's true that an isolated $200 chip-doping at a WSOP event is not going to dish out any big advantage to the forger. But that's hardly what was in the works. You can rest assured that the two players whose stacks contained the phony black chips had more of them on their person, to be invoked into their stacks if needed. It is also likely that other players in the tournament belonged to this chip-doping ring. Once word got out that two bad chips had been snatched up by the tournament's officials, the rest of them mixed into stacks on other tables disappeared quicker than a seashell rolled over by a tidal wave.

But it's not about measly black $100 tournament chips. In recent years poker's modern-day marketing has collided head on with its outlaw past, especially in megatournaments. What I'm saying is that these same chip-dopers hold reserves of fake tournament chips. They have purple $500 tournament chips; they have yellow $1,000 tournament chips; chocolate $5,000 tournament chips, whatever they need. They keep a multi-denomination stash of these phony tournament chips the same way I kept a stash of real $5,000 casino chips at the time I was doing huge pastposting moves up and down the Las Vegas strip.

As the WSOP uses the same chips for all its events, the arming of crooked players with bogus chips affords them a big advantage at the tables. Knowing that they never have to worry about getting snagged at the main casino cage trying to turn counterfeit chips into cash, which is a serious felony punishable by hard prison time, the tournament "chipsters" have found an ideal way to use their fake chips.

The key is to bring them into play in later rounds, when the betting limits increase to $1,000–2,000 and higher. A few extra chips in clutch situations can prevent a player from being knocked out of the tournament. If a team is working fake chips in collusion, one member can easily pass them off to another in need during the breaks. Since there are so many functions carried out by tournament personnel, they cannot worry about counting out everyone's chips during the break to ascertain no odd ones had been slipped into play.

Just how do the chipsters slide them into their stacks? Do they have to be sleight-of-hand artists and be able to palm chips? Well, those skills would help but are not necessary. The important element is to keep your bogus chips camouflaged in your legitimate stacks. If they're the same color as the legitimate chips and placed anywhere but at the top of the stack, no one will notice their existence in the game. The players caught in possession of the black tournament $100s had low quality fakes from the gift shop, one reason why the "I got them mixed up" theory holds water. In most chip-doping operations, the fakes sneaked into play are of much better quality and can withstand scrutiny as long as it's not being done with outright suspicion. It is not that difficult to counterfeit chips, and tournament chips do not undergo the stringent scrutiny that casino chips do when presented for payment at the cashier cage.

Let's say, for instance, that players A, B, C and D are working a phony-chip collusion scam at the WSOP. The particular event doesn't matter because it all works the same way. At the start of the tournament they are each armed with five phony $100 black chips. If the tournament's early betting limits begin at $25–50, then black chips are the right ones to have hidden initially in their stacks. Purple $500s or yellow $1,000s would serve no purpose during those stages of the tournament, except to get you 86'd from the event if one of those chips surfaced on the table before the tournament supervisors distributed them.

Let's assume that Player A takes a few early beats and is short chips. He now needs to get his phonies into play. Perhaps he had them in his stack since the outset of play, constantly covering them with his hands. In tournament play, players can do with their chips as they please, so long as none of them (visibly) leave the table. Most players do fiddle incessantly with their chips, shuffling and cutting them any which way they can, some of whom might be thinking they're regular in-house magicians. The overall effect of such rampant chip-play is to create a cacophony of pleasant chimes mixing effortlessly throughout the cardroom. This constant noise provides chip cheats with cover.

If Player A did not have his phony blacks buried in his stack and now needs to get them, he can fetch them easily from his person, though he must be careful. The trick is to get them in his palm (if they're not already there) and then gracefully merge them into his stack. He must make this move while he still has legitimate black tournament chips in play, and he must remember not to get caught going all-in when having only fake chips. That would be a sure way to get nabbed, as a player going all-in would have his chips scrutinized by both the dealer and opposing players wanting to ascertain how much in chips had to be matched. Experienced chipsters are more than capable of carrying out these functions with relative ease.

Now to further describe the utility of a chip-doping operation, let's have the first tournament break arrive. The players are given a short break during which they can go to the bathroom, grab a bite, a drink, or just bullshit on or off their cell phones or anything else they damn well please. During this particular break, however, Players A, B, and C have a pressing problem that must be dealt with: Player C is running out of chips and faces early elimination from the tournament. The one saving grace is that black $100 chips are still on the tables, therefore, Players A and B can rearm their buddy, so they do.

The next crucial step in the chip-doping conspiracy takes place when the limits are raised and the purple $500 chips appear. The players must rack their $100 chips and exchange them for purples. If their phony blacks are a decent match to the legitimate chips, both on their sides and in the center where the logo-design is, then the chipsters need not fear exchanging them straight out for the purples. It's likely that the bogus blacks would not be discovered because they're just tournament chips. The chance of a discovery like the one that happened at the Rio during the 2005 World Series would be minimal.

But if their phony chips risked sticking out when casually spilled among the real ones, they would do better to remove the fake chips from the tournament at that point. In either case it's time to bring out their reserves of fake purples. The chipsters would then mesh the phony purples into their purple stacks on the table in the same fashion they'd done with the blacks. During the following break they would furtively consult with one another to see which player, if any, needed more phony chips. The process would continue into the next rounds when yellow $1,000 chips were brought into play by the tournament supervisors. If the team of chipsters had high-quality fakes, they could sneak them into play right up until the final half-dozen or so tables in the tournament. At a certain time it might become too risky to venture using fake chips. As the tournament comes down to the wire and players are moving all-in at a rapid pace, the chips in front of the remaining players are subject to more scrutiny than during the middle rounds of the tournament.

The bogus-chip smuggling does not end with the conclusion of the tournament. The chipsters hold on to their reserves of phony chips for next year's WSOP. Normally the same series of tournament chips is used for some years running, and if new ones are introduced, there's nothing to stop the chipsters from counterfeiting them as well. The key is that the fake chips are never presented at the casino cage to be exchanged for cash, which in general protects the chip fraudsters from anything more serious than being expelled from the tournament and forfeiting their buy-in money.

Teams that use fake chips regularly take the trouble of counterfeiting tournament chips for all the major poker events worldwide. Each uses other forms of collusion cheating to enhance its edge. Phony-chip infusion alone, though advantageous, is not enough to really get a team over the hump where their investment-odds during an entire tournament would be favorable.

Due to the revelation of phony chips showing up at the 2005 WSOP, there's been talk of introducing radio frequency identification chips (RFID) into major tournament play. These are specially made chips with computer chips implanted in the center, where the logo is, that can be blipped onto monitors by surveillance people keeping track of the games. The idea for the RFID chips was originally conceptualized to allow casinos to monitor the action of their players, on which they could determine which players deserved comps, which were winning and not paying their markers, and even which were cheating. Personally I was very concerned when I heard about these RFID chips. If implemented at casino table games, they could identify the amount of money bet before the outcome of the event, which meant I would not be able to alter a bet after a hand had been dealt, the dice thrown or a roulette ball dropped.

But as of this writing, widespread use of RFID appears at best to be in the distant future. Presently the system is too expensive for casinos that stock millions of chips. There are a handful of casinos that are conducting trials with RFID chips right now, but they are limited and the idea does not appear to be catching fire anywhere. So into the near future, chipsters working the tournaments with counterfeit chips, whether they make them or just buy them in novelty shops, will be able to continue their operations.

Cheating in televised tournament events

Does cheating go on in televised tournament events, right in front of the cameras?

Wait a minute! You mean *before* they go in front of the cameras, don't you? While they're backstage with the makeup girl getting their faces buffed and agree to ham it up for the cameras, only to divvy up the prize money outside the studio moments after the announcers finish raving about the passionate competition. Come on, you don't believe that NBC poker "heads-up challenge" crap, do you? The only *challenge* is to make it all look good for the cameras. And why should the network care? If it looks good, the ratings go heads up.

Okay, what about *in front of* the cameras? Did you see the movie *Casino Royale*? Remember the scene with the shaded glasses Peter Sellers wore to see the marked cards through that greenish haze? If you've watched the Challenge TV series *Tilt*, remember the cheating scams the Matador and his crew pulled off. Well, I'm not saying they're good or bad, but they sure as hell are fictional.

What about *real* TV? Imagine this tense scenario: a final table in a televised World Poker Tour event and five players are seated at the table vying for the big prize money. Once again we have Players A, B, C, D and Player X. I'm going to jump out of alphabetical order for this situation simply for effect.

Of course the game is no-limit hold'em and the blinds are way up there, say $10,000–20,000. The chip distribution among the players is fairly level – $150,000–600,000.

The dealer deals the cards. Player C, under the gun in Seat 3, raises $60,000. Thanks to the tiny camera embedded underneath the table's surface, we see he's holding a pretty hand of A♠-Q♠. Player D calls. We see he's holding A-K offsuit. He could have raised but he's either slowplaying or wary of Player C, who might have a strong hand to go with his $60,000 raise.

Now we peek along with Player X at his cards. They're mediocre: a pocket pair of 6s. He takes a glance at the other players' chip-stacks and calls. Players A and B fold. Now we're treated to the exact percentage probabilities for each player to win the hand. Player X has a slight advantage over his two opponents.

The flop comes J♦-10♦-7♠. Player C, with the chip lead, comes right out and bets $100,000 as though he caught the flop. At this stage of the tournament, Player D does not like his hand after the flop and chucks it. Player X sees three over-cards on board higher than his 6s, plus two diamonds, of which he has none. But apparently he still likes his pair of 6s enough to call. He matches the 100 grand.

The turn comes J♠. The board now shows a pair of jacks with two spades and two diamonds. The percentages pop up on the screen next to the players' cards and names. We see that the odds favor Player X, 53% to 47%, even though his pair of 6s is not a strong hand. Player C checks to Player X. Player X fiddles with his chips, while the announcers discuss the strategies and possibilities in such a hesitant whisper that you might think tough poker decisions are as excruciating as Harry Truman's decision to drop the A-bomb on Japan.

After all that suspense, Player X simply checks back.

The river card is the 2♦. Player C smiles broadly at Player X, and even more broadly into the camera. He then asks Player X to tally the chips he has in front of him. The dealer counts out Player X's chips and informs the table that there is $180,000 in front of Player X. Player C cuts out $180,000 of his chips and makes the bet.

Player X is looking at a losing situation. He does have a pocket pair but there are three overcards on board. If Player C has a 7, 10 or jack in the hole, Player X loses. Even though the board paired with jacks, there is still the possibility, albeit small, that Player C has a third jack in the hole.

But judging by the way Player C came out so aggressively on the river, after the dealer turned the 2♦, Player X would have to put him either on a diamond flush or on a plain bluff. With 180 grand in chips left, he still has enough ammo to take an all-in shot with a better hand on a subsequent deal. We know that his pair of 6s is the best hand and that Player C played his smooth bluff to the hilt, but Player X does not know this.

Or does he?

He smiles back at Player C, pushes all his chips toward the center of the table and calls. He wins the pot and, just like that, is now chip leader for the tournament.

Why did Player X make such a gutsy call? Because like in the movies *Casino Royale* and *Goldfinger*, in which the man with the golden touch had a mole spying his opponent's hands through binoculars from a hotel balcony, Player X had his James Bond bug in his ear and heard a soft voice whisper, "He's got ace-queen suited; you win."

Could this happen? Well, I guess it could indeed if someone involved in the production of the show were in cahoots with Player X. Since the show is not beamed live into TV Land, it would be impossible for Player X's whisperer to be someone watching the broadcast, just as it would for someone viewing *Who Wants to be a Millionaire?* to transmit a million-dollar answer into a contestant's ear.

So let me deviate just one time from my supposition that there is corruption in poker *everywhere*. I will say that when a poker event is televised, apart from dirty deals made before the taping, there is absolutely no cheating going on at the table, not even collusion. They wouldn't be able to signal the values of their hole cards without risk of detection. Nor could they slip counterfeit chips into their stacks. They couldn't really do much of anything underneath those bright lights. But, of course, the endorsement value of their appearances takes care of everything.

Crooked fingers in WSOP ring games

Over the years during the World Series of Poker at Binion's Horseshoe, I've witnessed a great deal of cheating in tournament play. But the overall cheating was in no way confined to the gold-bracelet events.

Many tournament players who come from all over the world to vie for the championships are very wealthy individuals. They arrive in Las Vegas with big bankrolls. Most of them stick around for the duration of the month-long extravaganza. They play their fair share of events, though the majority doesn't play in every event. Naturally they can't make it to the final table of each and every event they enter (not even the cheaters can), so their exit from any given tournament might be quite early in the evening, even the afternoon. When they are fortunate enough to make it deep into the tournament, they still usually finish playing before midnight, with the exception of the championship event, which can drag on into the wee hours.

So what do you think these heavily armed poker players do when they're not actually involved in tournament play? I mean besides eating, drinking, catching a little sun (though this is not common among the pale-faced poker population) and sleeping?

They play poker, of course. Do not forget that the WSOP has plenty more to offer than its chartered events. It also stages the largest ring games seen anywhere in the world. Limit cash games can go as high as $5,000–10,000. Pot-limit and no-limit cash games can go right through the roof. Do you see where I'm leading? I've talked extensively about the tournament cheating syndicates. Now I'm going to talk about a branch of these syndicates that doesn't bother with the tournaments.

They beat the shit out of the huge cash games. They do it through collusion.

One early morning at two o'clock during the 2003 WSOP, I wondered over to the side-games area for a peek at the action. The no-limit hold'em tournament event had ended a few hours earlier. Many players who'd participated in the event were now engaged in crossfire action at a battlefield of green oval tables spread across the opened floor near the Horseshoe's sports book.

One table was separated from the others. An armed security guard stood like a prison wall at either end. Several more hung loosely around the table. When I took a closer look at the felt, I saw why. There were bricks on top of bricks in front of each of the four players. Yes, I'm talking about bricks of cash. Packets and packets of $100 bills rubber-banded to form each brick.

Three of the players were well-known high-stakes ring-game specialists based in Vegas. Two of them doubled as tournament players but had never been holders of gold-bracelets. The fourth player is the one who aroused my curiosity. He was a pioneering midwestern casino owner who had made his fortune long before venturing into casino partnerships with Indian tribes. He also had a very flamboyant personality.

As my suspicions about WSOP cheating had already been confirmed by firsthand observation of tournament events, I conducted my surveillance of this humongous ring game not with the idea that cheating may be going on but rather the mission of pinning down who was cheating whom and by what means.

They were playing $3,000–6,000 Texas hold'em, a huge game. Anyone caught in it while on a bad losing streak could go for half a million bucks. Somehow, before it became evident, I knew the casino owner would be the one in the game to get buried.

When I started watching the action, his pyramid of cash was both higher and wider than those in front of the three other players. I was standing 30 feet away, as close as you could get without being reprimanded by the security guards. I could not accurately count his money, but it looked to be in the neighborhood of a million bucks. When that visual calculation registered, my next thought was to leap over the stanchion enclosing the table, swoop up as much of the cash as I could, then run out the door and get out of Dodge. Only problem was I had nowhere to put the cash. Had I brought along a little gym bag or something, then maybe I could've taken the shot. A motorcycle outside with a getaway driver would have also come in handy.

After my fantastical thoughts subsided, I began intently watching the action on the table. Most of the pots unfolded quickly: the player under the gun folding; the player on the button raising; the blinds folding and the dealer pushing the $4,500 in chips to the winner. Such boom-boom-and-out poker was highly common in huge-limit games.

However, when the player under the gun called or raised, there followed staccato bursts of action and big pots. There was also a lot of re-raising taking place, especially when the casino owner was involved in the pot. I guessed that at such high limits in a short-handed game, camouflage was not deemed necessary. It appeared that each time the casino owner called a bet, the next guy raised and the guy behind him re-raised. When the casino owner raised, the threesome folded in tandem like a convoy of jackknifed trucks. It wasn't hard to see that the three wily pros were whipsawing the sawdust out of him.

By four o'clock in the morning I was getting tired. Besides, I'd seen enough. If I'd known then I was going to write this book, I might have hung around longer. But I'd stayed long enough and surely never forgot what I had seen. The casino owner's pyramid of cash had collapsed into a tee-pee. Perhaps he had 50 grand left when I walked out to Fremont Street and hailed a cab. I learned later that the guy lost $10 million over the years in WSOP ring games.

A few nights after witnessing that slaughter, I found myself back at the Horseshoe watching the same table. This time there were six players. Two of the three colluders from the first time were at the table. So was the casino owner. I looked around for the third colluder, who was missing. The last two tables of the day's tournament were still going, but he was to be found at neither. Perhaps he'd just taken the night off or was somewhere else hustling another game with another collusion team.

The three newcomers to the game included a flashy female Texan wearing a cowboy hat with an assortment of big diamonds wrapped around her fingers and necklaces around her décolletage that sparkled more than the chandeliers above the table. She was sandwiched between two wealthy Arab-types, and the three of *them* were sandwiched by three hardened Vegas colluders, one of whom I'd not previously seen.

I observed the action for two hours. They started off playing the same $3,000–6,000 hold'em, but half an hour into it they raised the stakes to $5,000–10,000, at the urging of the woman who had gone on tilt. To this day that game remains the biggest-money poker game I've ever seen. By the time it was over, the woman—who turned out to be the wife of a Texas oil man who never flirted with ring action but was a junkie for tournaments—lost nearly a million dollars. The two Arab guys went for a few hundred grand each. In all, it was a pretty hefty payday for the collusion team.

I actually felt sorry for the woman because she'd clearly been a victim. In fact, I wanted to approach her and tell her she'd been cheated, but doing so would have served only to get me back-roomed and interrogated by Horseshoe security. I certainly wasn't about to undergo that, knowing that once my presence was discovered by the Gaming Control Board, a whole investigation would take place just to find out what *I* was doing there.

In retrospect, I hope that rich lady-Texan reads this book. Maybe she'd change her Vegas ways and watch her husband play in WSOP tournaments instead of venturing into cash games to be eaten alive by the sharks.

My recommendation to you super high-rolling poker players with those tremendous wads of cash: if you're not part of the cliques playing the big-time side games at the WSOP, avoid them like the plague.

CHAPTER FOUR

WHY PROFESSIONALS CHEAT:
THE PSYCHOLOGY OF POKER CHEATING

For the sake of this argument, I am going to use the term "professional" for all people who play poker as a full-time occupation. This does not mean that they earn money playing. In reality, there are more "professional" poker players who consistently lose money than those who actually pay the bills by grace of their poker earnings, let alone the select 50 or so who've become household names.

One thing for sure is that competition is intense out there in the poker world. The desire to win and reach the pinnacle of the game is no less obsessive than in world sport, which is what poker has become, if we are willing to accept that poker coverage has cropped up in the sports pages of every major newspaper in the country.

Each day during the WSOP, you can find articles recapping the tournament's events on the front page of sports sections in most of the nation's influential newspapers. Weekly poker columns now appear in the *New York Times* and other distinguished papers. In short, today's top professional poker players are getting nearly as much press as Tiger Woods and Roger Federer. This is a far cry from the days not so long ago when poker arenas were sully back rooms in seedy taverns.

The game has since climbed to the top of the mountain, where it has gained classification as a highly respected social event and become topical enough to be played under the bright lights of movie sets.

But what about the full-time players who are not at the top? Those perhaps considered as the World Poker Tour's minor leaguers. Do you think for a second they don't envy the likes of players whose names we hear and read daily, that they're not downright jealous of those guys and gals who've reaped fame and fortune after turning $40 online tournament buy-ins into multimillion-dollar first-prizes and WSOP championships?

I can tell you this: my poker-playing buddy Preacher, who, by the way, considered himself as much a professional poker player as Tiger Woods does himself a pro golfer, was insanely obsessed by his drive to reach poker's heights. Other players I knew on the circuit displayed similar tendencies and emotions. They live, eat and breathe poker. They will go to any means to stay in action on the tournament circuit and reach the top. *Any means.*

This is where cheating comes in. In an imperfect world I will give you a perfect analogy. Let's compare poker to American baseball. In the American nation's first national pastime, though poker is clearly threatening it, we saw star players making $15 million or more taking steroids to enhance their performance. Okay, we understand why they took steroids, but why was enhancing their performance so damned important? If you're making that kind of money annually and all you have to do is go out each day and play a game that you loved as a kid, isn't that enough? Is it really necessary to abuse your body by taking steroids? Don't players who take steroids remember what former American football great Lyle Alzado looked like just before he died, his brain ravaged by steroid-induced cancer?

Obviously the answers to these questions defy logic. Some baseball players in constant search of glory and feeling the pressure, whether it's to win the World Series of that sport or to break monumental individual records, deem taking steroids as a necessary means to achieve their ends. If that's an indisputable fact, then can one deny the probability that certain professional poker players, either striving to reach the zenith of their own sport or simply bent on staying there, would resort to cheating the way athletes do by taking steroids?

If you think I'm just stirring up a cauldron of unfounded accusations, think again. Not only do some professional players cheat for the reasons I've already stated but others cheat simply to stay in the game. In baseball, certain players who've resorted to taking steroids did so only because their peers were doing it. Fearing that other power hitters would reach the 60-home-run plateau, previously clean power hitters didn't want to be left in the dust hitting only 40 or 50.

Same ideology in poker. When an honest major tournament player gets wind that cheating syndicates have been formed by other equally skilled players, he must contemplate involving himself in the same racket. To do so might be the only means of staying competitive, and when you're putting up 10 grand to enter a prestigious WSOP event, you don't want to get beat by those dirty rotten scoundrels teaming up against you. So sometimes, like the saying goes, it's better to join 'em than fight 'em. In order to understand this more fully, let's take a good, hard look at professional poker players, both as a group and as individual beings.

The psychological makeup of a professional poker player can be very complex and is often deeply layered. There is no doubt that he is a person of superior intelligence. There is no doubt that he is a special breed. There is also no doubt that he *knows* he's a special breed. To those few among them who aren't so self-assured, all they need to do is listen to the rest of the population talk about them. Am I wrong, or have today's top poker players been made over into celebrities whose nearly every move and tournament performance is splashed in newspapers and on television sets across the entire country? When will the first WSOP champion be motorcaded to 10 Downing Street to have his picture taken with the prime minister? Can't be too far away, even if that champion is not British-born.

There are certain characteristics that the majority of professional poker players seem to share. We all know about their egos. We also know how dedicated they are to the game and to making themselves the best they can be at it. But what remains hidden underneath their smooth veneers is *why* they became poker players. Why is it that tens of thousands of people, undoubtedly capable of making large amounts of money by way of more traditional occupations, dedicate their lives to sitting on their asses in smoke-filled or smokeless poker rooms, or in front of home computer screens, in the frenzied pursuit of removing other people just like them from their money?

If we examine the old-timers, say those at least 60-years-old, we could say they embraced the life of a poker player out of a genuine love for the game and a craving for its inherent gamble. Many old-timers came from backgrounds on the fringes of illegality. Some were just plain outlaws. Few ever had adult aspirations of joining traditional society. Among their population were many hard drinkers, womanizers and guys who just had a plain knack of finding troublesome situations. In all, players from this generation hold a palpable, almost proprietary nostalgia for poker as a lifestyle on the margins, an existence carved out in rough-and-tumble back rooms that is now obsolete.

Today's younger rat-pack-generation players come from a broader spectrum of life. We see ex-computer programmers, Wall Street whiz kids, small business owners and even ex-professional athletes (not to say that ex-athletes who used steroids are more apt to join the poker circuit than those who didn't). These younger guys, and now women, are very much attracted to the fast money big-time poker can provide them. Moreover, they don't have to report to anybody in the office and can work whatever hours they want.

Many young people play simply out of a rebelliousness toward society. Some play only to prove to their peers (or parents) how smart they are. No matter what each player's motivational force, all professionals, young and old alike, are bonded by two elements: ego and greed. Of course there are varying degrees to this, and a small percentage of players may possess neither of these negative characteristics. However, there is no doubt that gambling, in all its forms, attracts a less altruistic breed than say Red Cross volunteer work.

Many of the poker-playing faithful do not fully distinguish between what is honest and what is dishonest, in and out of a poker game. There is a definite connection between the strategic deception used by poker players in the heat of battle and their day-to-day lying outside the game. Perhaps the biggest lies professionals routinely tell concern their current financial position. How many times have you asked a poker buddy coming off a score for a little stake to get yourself back in action, only to hear him tell you he's broke? Or if he's not broke, his increased bankroll is already committed to this or that, and he only has enough disposable cash to get himself in a game.

Another occurrence of dishonest dealings constantly seen in the poker world is people welching on debts. Most poker players, with the exception of those who have scored big in major tournaments, occasionally find themselves on the rail watching the action instead of participating. The one and only reason for that is they've lost their stakes in action and gone broke. The only way these busted-out players can get back to the tables is to obtain loans from other players. This happens countless times each day, both in cardrooms and online.

But, unfortunately, poker debtors do not generally honor their debts with the same adherence that people outside the gambling world do. They often choose to deter money that had been earmarked to pay off loans into a poker game. This type of negligence is so common in the poker world that its effect is to create a revolving door of creditors chasing debtors chasing new prospective creditors. Such an undercurrent flowing through poker rooms helps breed an atmosphere that can stimulate rampant cheating.

In looking at calculated or premeditated strategies for cheating at top levels of professional poker, those unrelated to the ubiquitous desperation of players in urgent need of stake money, I will give you a nuts and bolts example of the collective benefit cheating provides to top tournament players.

Each year, the World Series of Poker brings the greatest and richest poker tournaments in the world to Las Vegas, Nevada. There is upwards of $100 million in prize money and who knows how much money is won and lost in the ring games going on 24/7 during the massive event. The top professional players who dominate the field at the WSOP all claim to be "poker players and not gamblers." If this were true then why would they gamble when they don't have to? By nature they would rather earn their fair share of the pot than risk losing it to possess the total pot.

And that's exactly what they do.

Most finalists in these grand events are live-game professionals who have been around cardrooms for years. Very few of these players have not been involved in public of these players have not been involved in public cardroom collusion schemes at some point in their careers, even if the extent of it was not more than occasional courtesy folds to help fellow pros steal pots from unknown amateurs. However, the vast majority of today's professionals have participated in collusion poker in a much more active role than that.

Few members of the professional cheating establishment would have qualms about forming the same type of collusion teams at the WSOP and other major tournaments; it's strictly to their benefit. Suppose at the final table of the WSOP championship we see three players remaining, two established pros who know each other and each other's play very well and an amateur who got there by way of an incredible lucky streak, bouncing out many top pros along the way. Each of the pros has invested $10,000 to enter the tournament. If top prize is $7,500,000, and second place and third places are $4,500,000 and $2,500,000, respectively, then $14,500,000 is up for grabs.

The two pros could look at this situation two ways. If they played it on the square, given the three players had around the same amount of chips at the time, each would have an expected prize-money value of about $4,833,333, based on the notion that each of the three players would have approximately the same short-term chances of finishing first, second or third. We arrive at that figure by simply dividing $14,500,000, the total prize money for the top three places, by three. Of course nearly five million bucks is a terrific payday, but is that to say that our two pros would accept it when they could easily secure even more?

By playing it on the square they would be gambling. Assuming each pro is evenly skilled and that the amateur has Lady Luck on his side, any of the three could finish first, second or third. But now let's suppose the two pros decide they'd rather not gamble. They would much prefer simply to maximize the return on their $10,000 investments. The best way to do this would be for them to gang up on the lucky amateur and assure themselves that he finishes third. Two colluding professionals knocking a third player out of a final tournament table is relatively easy to do. It would take some real bad luck not to be successful.

So by how much would this arrangement improve the pros' investment-odds? A third-place finish for the amateur would pay him $2,500,000 and leave $12,000,000 to be split up between the pros. That comes to $6,000,000 apiece, more than a million bucks greater than their individual expected values and *three and a half* million more than what each would receive on finishing third. So, in effect, the difference between colluding and not colluding is a guaranteed $3,500,000 excess profit in the pockets of the two pros. I can't believe there are many who would not opt for that outcome, less so if they need the money.

You think *this* is blatant? What about high-stakes shoot-out tournaments where the winner gets all the cash and the run-ner-ups get pats on the backs and handshakes from the win-ner? Do you think our two pros would even consider not col-luding in that situation?

Let's drop the stakes a little and say the two pros and lone amateur are at the final table of a winner-take-all $1,000,000 shoot-out. In this scenario the pros would be even less in-clined to give it a go on the square. Why? Because if the ama-teur wins they both go home with nothing more than a jacket and ball cap from the tournament sponsor. But if they pool their skills and resources, each stands a very high chance of winning half a million bucks. So what would *you* do after having come so far to reach the final table of this tournament? Take the 500 grand or buck a two-thirds probability of going home with just the shirt on your back?

So what we see is that even the best of poker professionals embrace the opportunity to protect their investments by way of colluding with other poker professionals looking to do the same. These players are merely adopting to the system the same way baseball players, in spite of the reluctance of many of them, adopted to theirs. Collusion has become a trade tool required for playing competitive professional poker at its highest levels. In some cases, it's actually a vehicle for survival on a cutthroat professional tour.

Those players who practice collusion but find it repugnant probably justify it with a sense of professional righteousness. Those who cannot surmount the moral obstacle probably end up doing something else for a living.

Why do honest players who know cheating is going on all around them continue playing poker?

I remember a very enlightening experience I had in the company of an inveterate gambler named Phil. It was a crisp fall evening and we were at Yonkers Raceway for a night of harness racing, which has seen its share of gambling scandals and is widely considered to be crooked.

I was basically along for the ride, horse racing never being one of my gambling attractions. I noticed Phil intently studying his *Daily Racing Form* as though he were analyzing a scientific formula. He was torn between two horses for the upcoming race.

"Phil, let me ask you something," I said with curious amusement. "Everyone and his uncle know that these harness races are all fixed. So why the hell do you waste your time trying so hard to figure out which horse is gonna win?"

Phil, who is 15 years my senior, gave off a condescending smile. Then with the brightness that most degenerate gamblers possess, he paralleled his favorite author, Sir Arthur

Conan Doyle, in explaining it to me. "My dear Watson," he said in lofty but serious tones, "you are absolutely right that all these godforsaken races are as fixed as your horoscope, but that doesn't matter worth a damn."

I looked at him somewhat vaguely.

"You see," continued Phil, "that the race is fixed only matters when you know exactly how the fix is in. If you know the 3-horse is going to win, then it matters. But since I *don't* know which horse has been fixed to win, then it's the same as if the race hasn't been fixed at all." He paused to see if his logic sunk in. "You see what I'm saying?"

I certainly did. Phil's philosophy was of solid ground; it made sense. If the outcome of a basketball game is fixed and you're a gambler looking to predict the outcome without knowledge as to which way the fix went in, then you should simply ignore the fix and handicap the game according to your set criteria. The reasoning is that if you don't know the direction of the fix, then it's a 50–50 chance the fix went with you or against you. Likewise in a horse race with multiple horses, the fix does not affect the odds of your horse winning the race when you're in the dark. If it's a 10-horse field and one horse has been made to win by the fix, the odds that it's your horse is 9–1, but it's irrelevant because you don't know it. I had no trouble understanding Phil's theory. It was kind of a gambler's "ignorance is bliss."

So how does this apply to honest poker players pursuing ring games even though they know there's cheating? Well, the fixed-race analogy applies to poker but is only a piece of the riddle. Lots of honest poker players have the attitude that cheating is always going to be present, so it's just an added tangible of the game that has to be overcome. They might look at cheating as a 10th opponent sitting among the other nine in a full game. That outlook is certainly commendable as long as the players supporting it don't entertain the idea of trying to beat the cheat at his own game. If they strive to make enough money off legitimate players in order to overcome losses incurred to cheats, then their strategy flies.

Many authors have endorsed a dealing-with-cheating theory in their books that absolutely enrages me, so false and pretentious is its claim. They say that not only are the majority of poker cheaters such bad players that they give away more in edge than what they make up for by cheating, but also that by playing smarter and more deceptive yourself, you can overcome these cheaters and their methods, without cheating, and actually beat them at the table!

Who are these authors trying to con? I've read stuff online where some poker guru goes out on a poker-playing tour with the purpose of encountering all kinds of cheaters and then challenges himself to read their scams and beat them at it without cheating back. Sounds great, doesn't it? Sure, I would agree. Maybe with the colossal popularity of poker it would make a great new TV series. It could even be called "Beat a cheat." You could have an expert poker player walk menacingly into a saloon-style cardroom, knocking open the swinging doors like James Coburn used to do in commercials, and sit down and announce to the conclave of cheaters gathered around the table, "I'm Mr. Wipe-A-Cheat. Gimme your best shot and watch me deflect it and take your money."

Sound ridiculous? It is. Take it from me: I was a cheater for a long time and no casino ever beat me.

Another reason honest players stay in the game with dishonest ones is that they simply can't help themselves. I am not going to pull any punches in saying that poker has become society's newest hard drug. It can be as addictive as any vice known since the inception of human indulgence.

Just look at what's going on online. Executives locked

inside their offices playing online poker is not an example of healthy leisure time. On college campuses across the country, poker has become bigger than sports. It's no longer "Come on, big guy, it's Saturday, let's get over to the homecoming game!" Rather it's "Leave me the fuck alone, I'm playing online poker!"

So it's difficult to believe that the knowledge of cheaters operating online is going to curtail those diehards from playing. Same theory applies to brick and mortar cardrooms. The masses of live poker-playing faithful are not about to fold up camp because cheaters are crashing the campfire.

Chapter Five

The Evolution of Poker Cheating:
A History of Who Cheats and Why

Do you know what the game of poker was called before it was called poker? If you don't, it might surprise you, but the original game was called "the cheating game." It was dealt with only 20 cards but the ranks of hands were basically the same.

Cheating at poker is as old as the game itself. The origins of poker are difficult to pinpoint, though many learned persons believe they can be traced to China around the year 950 AD. Others think the game originated from a 16th-century Persian card game called "As Nas," which was played with a 25-card deck containing five suits and whose rules were similar to today's five-card stud.

A variant of poker was first widely played in the United States in the early 1800s by French settlers in New Orleans. Soon afterwards it caught on with London's East End villains playing in back room venues. The French called the game "poque" and it was similar to the draw poker we play today, with lots of betting and bluffing. At about the same time, Louisiana hustlers began playing three-card monte, the cheating game in which the crook displays two black aces and one red ace, then turns the three cards face down and scrambles them, while his shills egg you on to believe it's a cinch to follow the red ace. But when you put up your money eagerly turning a card, it's one of the black aces and you lose.

New Orleans soon evolved into America's first gambling city. Riverboat men, plantation owners, farmers, restaurateurs all converged on the city to actively pursue the betting sport. The first actual American gambling casino was opened in the city in 1822 by a man named John Davis, an honest business man who doubled as a card cheat. Other casinos quickly opened, establishing the city and its international port as a thriving gambling industry. Out of this grew a new profession called the card "sharper," which was nothing short of a cheat.

Practitioners of this new profession and legitimate gamblers gathered in a waterfront area known as "the swamp," an area even the police preferred to avoid. Cheaters fleeced their victims in one of two ways. Either they got their money by dealing crooked games or simply robbed the lucky ones who survived the game on their way home.

The first hands of poker dealt on Mississippi riverboats used a 20-card deck containing 10s, jacks, queens, kings and aces. The first games of modern-day poker using 52-card decks were also staged along the banks of the Mississippi. Cheating was widespread among the finer southern gentlemen spending their days at poker tables on paddlewheel boats trudging up the great river. Many scams flourished but much of the early cheating was based on taking advantage of novice players not knowing the rules.

When poker became a game with a 52-card deck, not all of its players immediately grasped that three of a kind beat two pair or a flush beat a straight. Many of the suckers falling for the three-card-monte scam became poker's earliest pigeons. Those dumb enough to be conned into thinking they could pick the red ace among two black ones were the same fools whom sharpies convinced a straight beat a flush and two pair beat three of a kind. Many wealthy plantation owners with little gambling sense made plump victims for the scores of hustlers scouring riverboats in search of their prey.

Five-card stud and draw were the first popular poker games dealt in 19th-century New Orleans. Cheaters preferred draw because by the very nature of the game, players held the five cards dealt to them. Once the cheaters had the cards in their possession, they could use numerous sleight-of-hand tricks to vastly improve their hands. One simple trick that was hardly sleight-of-hand was to draw three cards while only discarding two, keeping the extra card high in the palm. The cheater could then hold that extra card tucked in his palm until he needed it to improve a hand, at which time he would simply slide it out and replace it with another card he would keep palmed until the opportune moment arrived to feed that one into his hand. In this fashion the cheater conducted a kind of revolving door of sixth-cards in a five-card game.

As commerce developed along the waterways, gambling and cheating travelled up the Mississippi and Ohio rivers, then westward via covered wagons and finally by railroad. In river towns popular to both travelers and gamblers more casinos opened up. The sharpers preyed mercilessly on these transient people, removing their life savings which were literally stashed in their pockets. Poker was just one of a warren of confidence games and con artist flimflams used to gaff unwary pioneers.

Another business that flourished along with the cheaters was the manufacturing of cheating devices, which commanded a hefty price. One riverboat cheater named George Devol was so proud of his ability to slip a stacked deck into a game that he once used four of them in one poker hand, dealing four aces to each of his four opponents. He said afterward that it was a joke just to show everyone who'd heard of the Louisiana Purchase how good he was.

Although it was true that Devol was a braggart who liked to tell everyone that his skull was an inch in thickness over his forehead, and that it had protected him from scores of terrible blows he received on his head from irate losers, he was also the greatest poker cheater in the history of the Mississippi River. At the age of 10, Devol, a delinquent kid, ran away from home and got a job on a steamer called the *Wacousta*. It was onboard the vessel that he got his first look at poker. His next boat job was on a better paddlewheeler called *Walnut Hills*. Aboard that boat he learned to play "seven-up," and increased his skills in the art of bluffing—and stealing poker chips. After a short stint on his second boat, Devol, then a teenager, landed a job on the luxurious *Cicero*, a steamer that carried the well-to-do of New Orleans.

Devol's calling in life came to him on the decks of the *Cicero*. Seeing the high lifestyle of well-heeled gamblers strolling the decks and poker rooms with beautiful women in tow, the young lad was determined to follow in their footsteps. He befriended a fellow worker on the boat who was a few years his senior and a half-decent manipulator of playing cards. This man was only too happy to show his protégé a few tricks.

By the time he was 15, Devol could very skillfully deal seconds, palm cards and recover the cut after a player was satisfied that his cut insured against any cheating on that hand. He then taught himself how to stack a deck, arranging the cards so that the following deal would bring his opponent a good hand but himself a better one. He was able to do this by recognizing patterns of cards from a previously played hand,

hand, then stacking them on the bottom of the deck and bringing them to the top via a series of perfected shuffles, riffles and cuts. He did those moves with an incredible agility and practiced them like a dedicated violinist did his music.

During the Mexican War, Devol enlisted and got a job bartending on the *Corvette*, a transport boat that took soldiers to the Rio Grande. He quickly set about using his repertoire of skills to swindle other soldiers, a custom that many crooked military men would follow throughout every American and British war. George succeeded in draining the soldiers' Army pay and steadily filled his pockets with bulges of ill-gotten gains. When the soldiers finally ran out of poker money, he returned to New Orleans.

Continuing to hone his skills, Devol met up with other cardsharps who would become nearly as notorious as he. Their names were Canada Bill Jones, Bill Rollins, and Big Alexander. They formed a partnership and worked the southern steamboats. Devol no longer needed a legitimate job to supplement his thieving income; he was doing quite well with his new partners. But soon their egos and jealousies got the best of one another and each took to cheating his three partners, mostly by holding out money when it came time to divvy up profits rather than at the card table.

Devol went back out to work his own sting. He had developed an unseemly reputation but was still able to hook businessmen, farmers and non-poker-cheating thieves into his rigged game. In spite of all his wanton conning of people, Devol developed a peculiar affinity for ministers. After beating them out of their meager wages, he gave the ministers their money back with the admonition "Go and sin no more." Devol never told anyone why he felt so unselfish toward men of the church, but perhaps the great con man had a conscience gnawing away at him.

When the war was over, the Union's railroads began heading west with settlements sprouting up along the way. Many of these burgeoning towns, often filled with rail workers, miners and cowboys, provided tons of opportunities for the accomplished cheater. George set out to follow this railroad expansion and prospered greatly as it turned into a golden yellow-brick road.

While working the Gold Room Saloon in Cheyenne, Wyoming, Devol encountered the legendary Wild Bill Hickok, an ex-sheriff who Devol swore was a cheat himself. After either being out-cheated or out-played by Hickok, Devol, extremely sore at losing his stake money, pointed his finger at Hickok and in a snarled voice growled, "One day you will be killed at a poker table!"

In 1892, Devol retired from gambling and actually published his autobiography, *Forty Years a Gambler on the Mississippi*. However, Americans on the whole weren't interested in reading about a notorious poker cheat (I hope they are now!). The book didn't fare very well, so Devol favored going back to poker. His wife insisted that he do nothing of the kind and keep trying to sell his book. Doing so door-to-door turned up very little money for the gambler-cheater who'd won and stole an estimated $2 million in his lifetime, a fantastic figure for the times. George Devol died in Hot Springs, Arkansas, in 1903. He was nearly penniless.

Cheaters like Devol are much responsible for America's first poker boom of the 19th century. And they were quite proud of it. They considered themselves as entrepreneurs, although many were illiterate. But they knew how to take advantage of the public. Whatever they lacked in formal education, they made up for by cultivating irresistible personalities and charm. They used those qualities to attract suckers to their games. Like their victims, they dressed in dandy clothes, knowing their success depended on making the people being fleeced feel comfortable in their company. The idea was to look as much like your suckers as possible.

Of course the suckers weren't fooled every time. One celebrated story serves as a good example of this. In 1832, right in the middle of riverboat gambling's heydays, four men were playing high-stakes poker on a Mississippi steamboat. Three were professional cheats. The fourth was an innocent and naïve traveler from an unspecified southern territory. The three cheaters used basic methods to cheat their victim, mainly dealing cards off the bottom of the deck and holding out extra cards in five-card draw.

Soon the hapless gambler lost all his money to the cheats— $50,000, and he was devastated. After a huge rigged pot, he suddenly jumped up from the table and ran to the boat's railing. He climbed up and was ready to cast himself into the river, a sure death by drowning. But another man who'd been lounging nearby grabbed him and pulled him safely back onto the deck. When this stranger learned why the gambler wanted to commit suicide, he became very upset.

The stranger decided to test out the game for himself. He sat down among the three cheats and took a hand. A few deals later, he spotted one of the cheats holding out a card from the deck. He wasted no time calling him on it.

"Show your hand!" he demanded of the cheat, pulling a knife on his throat. "If it contains more than five cards I shall kill you!"

The cheat resisted but the stranger twisted his arm within an inch of breaking it. Six cards fell to the table. The stranger cold-cocked the cheat and scooped up all the cash on the table. There was $70,000 between the pot and the cheaters' stake money. He counted out $50,000 and gave it to the suicidal victim. He kept $20,000 for his trouble.

Shocked, but now buoyed by the return of his life savings, the novice gambler asked the stranger, "Who the devil are you, anyway?"

The stranger replied, "I'm James Bowie."

That same James Bowie, who was quite lethal with a knife, later became co-commander of the Alamo. He died in the Battle of the Alamo in 1836.

Things began to get rough for southern cardsharps. Fisticuffs began breaking out regularly in gambling dens and saloons. In 1835, a group of enraged citizens in Vicksburg, Mississippi, lynched five hustlers who'd been caught cheating poker games. The collective disdain for card cheats and gambling bandits grew to the point where citizens began blaming them for every crime in the area, even those without the slightest connection to gambling. Violence over crooked card games continued to rise until finally cooled by the outbreak of the Civil War.

At the war's end, America pushed her boundaries west, where new frontiers born of speculators, travelers, miners and gold-rushers took foothold in her tracks. Many of these hardy pioneers were rough and tumble men and high-risk-takers with a thirst for gambling activity. In most of the mining camps and prairie towns scattered west of the plains were saloons whose poker tables sported prospectors, lawmen, cowboys, railroad workers, soldiers and, of course, outlaws. The honest workingmen were only chasing the chance to tempt fortune and fate, while the grifters were looking to rob them blind.

The violence surrounding poker cheating escalated rapidly in the Wild West. It took little time before that violence resulted in outcomes like the one that gave name to "the dead man's hand."

For those of you unfamiliar with that story, it happened on

August 2, 1876, in the Silver Dollar Saloon in Deadwood, South
Dakota. On that fateful day, Wild Bill Hickok, the legendary
ex-sheriff outlaw, was playing draw poker and got accused of
cheating. In the ensuing argument, one of the onlookers at the
bar, a man named Jack McCall who had held Hickok responsible for the death of his brother, whipped out his six-shooter,
stepped behind Wild Bill and shot him in the back of the head.
At the time of his death, Wild Bill held a pair of aces and a pair
of 8s in his hand. There is, however, a discrepancy over what
the fifth card was, but the two-pair hand of aces and 8s came to
be known as "the dead man's hand." An eerie footnote to Wild
Bill Hickok's murder was its premonition through the mouth
of George Devol some years before.

Those typical poker-table shootouts we've all seen countless times in westerns actually did happen as much as we saw
them. Poker players in the Wild West were a completely different breed from players you see today. They were rough
and tough cowboys who always had weapons on their hips
and weren't afraid to use them. Sometimes they were outright
trigger-happy. Oftentimes the fastest, most efficient way to
resolve a dispute at the poker table was to draw a gun and
open fire. But first you had better have some evidence. Shooting an innocent poker player to death was worse than rus-
tling cattle.

Fortunately, most crooked poker players who got themselves killed in a poker game were just that: crooked poker
players. On their dead bodies in front of witnesses, the cowboy who "done the shooting" would find the evidence of
cheating needed to prove he was justified in slaying the local
cheat, at least in the eyes of those at the poker game. But you
can bet as well that if the hanging judge occupied one of the
wooden chairs around the table, he wasn't about to have the
killer's ass hauled off to jail.

Each and every time, with few exceptions, that evidence was crude and blatant. It usually consisted of a card up a sleeve, attached to some type of spring or just stuffed in the crook of a cheater's elbow. These early card-muckers usually removed a card from the game and kept it hidden until they needed it. Sometimes they brought a card from a matching deck to the game from wherever they had obtained it—often at the same table the night before.

These games abided by lawlessness, hence there was no need to worry about being held back by the established rules and routines you see in cardrooms today. There was no automatic deck-change after 30 minutes. There was no designated dealer; the players dealt themselves, passing the deck around the table after each hand. While dealing, players were not required to follow any specific set of procedures. Nor were they required to burn cards from the top of the deck. About the only procedure rigorously adhered to was offering the player on your right the opportunity to cut the cards.

Card-marking scams also proliferated in the Wild West, although not to the extent of holding out cards. Cowboys used crude methods to mark the cards. One of the most popular was to glue a small piece of sandpaper to the underside of a finger. Then while handling the cards the cheater sanded down a small part of their backs in certain spots. One "sanding" cowboy who was caught with a tiny piece of sandpaper between his fingers denied using it to scratch the cards. When he was pressed to explain his actions, the barrel of a Colt .45 pressed against his temple, he said he'd been sanding down one of the wooden legs of the table that had a sharp edge constantly scraping his shin. The guy on the other side of the Colt promptly squeezed the trigger.

Some crooked cowboys who happened to fancy the sun used its rays to help them cheat at poker. A favorite ploy of card-markers was to take out the big cards from a deck and bake them in the sun for a few hours, after which they'd be faded. The key was to leave the aces in the sun the longest so that their backs would lose the most color, whereon the kings, queens, jacks and 10s were fetched out of the sun at intervals corresponding to desired fading levels. Since everyone brought their own "lucky" cards to saloon poker tables, each player had an equal opportunity to doctor up his deck. There were no magical, disappearing solutions in the days of the Wild West, but crooked cowboys did their best to be innovative.

Crooked cowgirls, too. The ones who were well endowed often used their "natural" tools of the trade to help out their favorite cowboys. Bending over in short skirts at the opportune moment was a surefire way to get suspicious eyes off whoever was performing the cheating move. Sometimes it was a bit clumsy trying to remove an ace stashed up a sleeve, therefore, the cowboy needed a little distraction so he could slide his hand up his arm and retrieve it. Sometimes the woman doing the bending, or making her chest expand at the right moment, delivered an errant card to a cowboy who might have fumbled trying to get it in or out of the game and inadvertently dropped it in the sawdust.

Women with big chests and poker scams seemed to go together. If one such woman was inside a saloon where a poker-table shootout occurred but not actually involved in the dispute, you can bet your case money she was soon to become the beneficiary of the disputed sum in one way or another. Many cowboys only needed the affections of large-chested women as motivation to risk their asses cheating.

From the Wild West, poker cheating, already deeply ingrained in the game, followed the course of history. Cheating soldiers from the Mexican war fathered sons who became cheating soldiers in the First World War who in turn fathered the next generation of cheating soldiers in the Second World War. That lineage of cheating descendants passed through Korea and Vietnam as well. Soldiers fighting every American war spent much of their leisure time playing poker and, in contrast to what many believe, the stakes were not only cigarettes. They were cold hard cash, whether it be Mexican pesos, French francs or Korean wons.

It is an accurate assumption that of all the men who have learned how to cheat at poker, more than 50% of them learned the various techniques while in the armed forces. As for women who learned these crafts, the vast majority of them learned from veterans of the armed forces.

There is a colorful poker-cheating story that came out of the Korean War. A platoon leader named Lieutenant Jason was particularly hard on one of his buck-privates named Hogan. With no apparent provocation, the lieutenant scolded the private on his whims. Another of Jason's habits was playing poker with his men. He constantly played poorly and whenever his losses piled up too high, Hogan, who wasn't even in the game, took the brunt of the lieutenant's frustration.

Near the end of a humiliating march during which Jason ridiculed Hogan, the private hatched an idea that would win so much favor with the lieutenant that Jason might put him in for a promotion. He approached the lieutenant as soon as the platoon returned to camp.

"Sir, I have an idea how to improve your poker game," Hogan began timidly.

"What the hell do you know about poker!" snapped Lieutenant Jason, in no mood to deal with the private.

"Well, not much, sir, but I think I know how to make you win."

Jason didn't really want to hear it but he'd recently lost an amount that exceeded his monthly pay.

The next platoon game was played later that afternoon. Hogan, a botany freak since childhood, was skilled at climbing trees. He found an easy one high above the campground where the soldiers played poker. He climbed it half an hour before the start of the game, his binoculars strapped around his neck. No one noticed.

The tree was just feet from their makeshift poker table. From his perch above, Hogan could look through the binoculars and clearly read the cards of each player whose back was toward him. Sometimes he could read the hands of players sitting at 90-degree angles to him as well. In all, he could supply his lieutenant with enough information to destroy the poker game.

The ingenious method Hogan used to signal Lieutenant Jason the value of his opponents' cards was to shake the branches of the trees. Jason would look up at the swaying branches and receive the data needed to play his hand. The first day they worked the scam, it went off like a charm. The next two days worked equally as well, but the following day it was very windy and Jason too often got Hogan's signals mixed up with the wind. From then on, Jason would only play when there was nothing more than a slight breeze.

After two months of scamming his men for their wages, Jason put Hogan in for a promotion. The rest of the platoon couldn't understand why, but what perplexed them even more was the sudden emergence of the lieutenant's poker skills. They just couldn't beat him and it seemed like Jason's winning streak would go on forever.

Perhaps it would have, but one fateful day brought a lightning-quick end to their scam. The game started out underneath a beautiful blue sky with absolutely no breeze. But then a sudden storm rolled in out of nowhere. The soldiers, in appreciation of the rapidly darkening sky, had agreed to play only one more hand. Hogan, in the tree, wanted to get down quickly but had to wait until the rest of the platoon cleared out.

An instant later, a lightning bolt struck the tree. Hogan fell out of it and landed smack in the pot.

One of the soldiers called. Another raised.

Private Hogan never returned from Korea.

CHAPTER SIX

ONLINE ONCRIME

You boot up your computer, you click the mouse a few times, and like magic you're in a poker game with people from all over the world in the virtual stratosphere. But is it safe?

The answer is "not always."

I am going to examine two sectors of Internet poker: the websites that supply you with the games and the faceless people throughout the world whom you play against. I have heard many online players express concerns about the integrity of online poker. Some fear being cheated by other players, who, they think, might be computer hackers with talents for writing programs that allow them to actually see their opponents' hole cards. Others don't trust the very sites. In the knowledge that many online poker's pioneers came from questionable entities suggesting track records of impropriety, they ask themselves, "How can one be sure that these sites don't use their own computer software to rip off its players?"

These kinds of concerns are understandable given the fact that the founder of PartyPoker.com, the largest gambling website online, made her initial ingress into the Internet poker world via online pornography.

How secure is the internal system?

Let's take a look at how the actual games offered by every online poker site work. They use random number generators (RNGs) to "shuffle and deal" the cards. In principle, unless they are crooked or contain bugs, computer shuffles are closer to being completely random than shuffles in a live action game. This is true because no cardroom dealer performs a totally random shuffle. He cannot obtain that result because he is human and often might just rush the shuffle to the point he is doing nothing more than riffling through the deck, leaving clumps of cards throughout.

However, there can be bugs in the shuffling algorithms. A few years back, a team of computer programmers from Silicon Valley moonlighting as card cheats discovered a means of calculating the precise order of cards in decks shuffled by algorithms used by multiple online cardrooms. Their discovery was hushed, but the fact was that with the application of this knowledge, the cheats knew in advance the hand of each player at the table as well as the future cards to be dealt: either to the players individually in stud games or on board in hold'em and Omaha games. The flaw in the algorithm was that the starting point used for the RNG was the number of milliseconds since midnight according to the system's clock. All the Silicon Valley geeks had to do to compromise the RNG was synchronize their program with the system clock. Online cardrooms today insist it is no longer possible to crack their shuffling algorithms, but I wouldn't want to bet my case money on what they say.

If RNGs are truly random, then over millions of hands we should see a distribution of deals, flops, turns and rivers no different than live poker. But I have heard from many sources in the know that the RNG's randomness may not be 100% random. A computer whiz I know has run his own programs to keep track of what goes on in Internet poker. He chose one particular major site and tracked a million hands of Texas hold'em. What he found, somewhat to his shock as he professed it to me, was that the RNGs seemed to be skewed to put more pairs on board and create more flush draws. Although such machination is not directly cheating its playing customers, it certainly can be concluded that biased RNGs benefit the site immensely.

How? The obvious explanation is that they create more action. When you have an inordinate number of flush draws, you keep more players looking to catch a flush in the pot. Same thing with pairs on board. They open up possibilities of sets and full houses. Again, more players exhibiting more staying power creates a lot more action. The end result is the creation of bigger pots, which in turn attracts more players to the site, increasing its revenues through table rakes of more games. Do I personally believe this is still happening on the major sites?

You bet. Even if the RNGs are skewed by just a tiny amount, let's say a fraction of 1%, that irregularity will generate millions of dollars of additional revenue for the site over a long period of time. As for the players, they are not being cheated directly, but the vast majority are losing more money, simply because they're playing more pots and staying deeper in those pots as the RNGs consistently offer more outs on both the turn and the river.

I have also been made aware of further, more serious concerns expressed by online poker players. Many sites use prop players to get more tables in action. This is an old, tired trick used by Las Vegas casinos and cardrooms since Nevada legalized gambling. Supposedly these props are paid an hourly rate or get reimbursed a portion of the rake. The sites claim they have no interest in whether their props win or lose. But could there be more to this?

Allegations have been made that the sites have used software with special programs that distribute an inordinate percentage of winning hands to its props, who, if one wants to believe are more than simple props, rake in money not for themselves but for the site. This kind of bias would be nothing short of major cheating, and if any online poker room were guilty of it and found out, the site would surely lose all its business and subject its officers to hordes of legal problems, the least of which would be simple loss of license.

Do I think online poker rooms engage in this kind of active cheating?

No. Today's major sites would have too much to lose. But I will not go as far to say that they *never* resorted to such tactics. In the early days of Internet poker, some of the innovators were desperate to be successful at it. They knew it was a hit or miss deal and they had to launch big numbers fast. They were fearful of how little time they would have to get rich. After all, legislation had begun in the United States, where 90% of their clientele is based, to permanently outlaw Internet gambling in all its shapes and forms. This febrile attack by state prosecutors' offices is still swarming the Internet's beachheads, but as of this moment the virtual poker rooms are holding down their forts.

In the beginnings of all that "gambling.com," providers of these controversial services did not have millions of business people all over the world missing meetings in order to play online poker and casino games, nor did they have millions of college students cutting classes to join the fray. In fact, at the advent of Internet gaming there were only a few thousand diehards willing to risk their money on a computer screen.

There was also a lot less software designed to monitor what was going on within the sites. About the only people developing programs capable of monitoring online gambling activity were the very programmers hired by the sites to install their software. Thus in the infancy of online poker, it was quite uncommon for independent people to keep track of the millions of hands needed to make an accurate analysis of statistical deviation and then apply it.

In conclusion, I will say that probably all the poker sites existing at the inception of Internet gaming practiced hanky-panky to some degree in order to ensure their survival. If not for that reason, then they "dealt seconds" to guarantee they would make a quick killing before the legislative American giants put the clamps on.

What about today? I would say that as far as props are concerned, all the big sites are generally clean (which doesn't mean the same holds true for biased RNGs that induce more action). Let's face it: it would be ridiculous for online cardrooms to jeopardize their licenses and billion-dollar businesses over crooked props. You've all heard that PartyPoker recently raised $9 billion from its initial public stock offering in London. Nine billion dollars! And that's only a fraction of the corporation's worth. Does anyone really believe that its officers, all billionaires, are going to fuck around when they've got something like that going? Hardly. Not unless they want to distribute those billions among every barrister in England.

On the other hand, hundreds of smaller online gambling entities have risen from the ashes of nowhere to fight for their share of the Internet market. Although it's unlikely any of them engage in cheating activities, it is still more probable that you would find some kinds of improprieties with these newer, less established online gaming vehicles. Even if it's only that they're a little slow in the drawer when you win.

Let's get to the meat and potatoes of online cheating. The second part of my discussion dealing with dishonesty in

Internet poker demands much more attention. That's because it goes on in a BIG way. It's all about collusion, but now I'm talking about collusion with the aid of computers, which is highly effective. Imagine what a school of computer sharks swimming in collusion could do to you honest players in online waters. They won't need the sight of your blood to propel their attack. They've got more hardware and ways to use it than a crab has claws. It is easier for them to cheat on the Internet than it is for the most skilled professional card-sharps to cheat in live poker rooms. What makes it that way?

First of all, they don't have to worry about signalling the values of their hands to one another. They do this via Instant Messenger or plain old telephone. It doesn't matter if their cohorts are in China or sitting right next to them. And imagine if there are four or five of them in one game. What about six or seven, or even eight or nine and you're the only person not in collusion against you? Sound absurd?

It's not. In high-stakes online games, it is well worth it for a team of poker-playing computer cheat-geeks to go after a single victim willing to part with a few grand, or at least willing to be connived out of his money. And once they're done with you, which happens much faster than in live poker, the piranha-geeks will bust out the next Internet sucker coming along while your cyber seat is still warm.

Now, before we go on, let me clear up a few things that have been erroneously preached to you by other authors, columnists and just plain top players who refuse to say, write or do anything that might give poker a bad name. When discussing allegations of cheating on the Internet, these *denialists* are real whippersnappers in telling you why you *think* you got cheated instead of affirming the truth, which is you *did* get cheated. I once overheard a young hotshot poker author tell a suspicious online loser that the reason he thought he got cheated was his failure to keep records of his cheated was his failure to keep records of his live table play. He actually said, "When you get your monthly credit card bill and realize that you've actually lost, you then realize in turn that all those times you thought you were beating the live games, you were losing as well."

Do you believe that crap? I sure as hell don't. I don't need some nerdy wiseass telling me that had I gone into the California cardrooms with a notepad, I wouldn't be suspicious of those online pricks cheating my pants off. No thanks.

Then you get the nonbelievers who tell you stuff like "You get wiped out online because you're never concentrating totally while playing. You're either watching TV, listening to music or getting laid. Or all three at once." Or then, they assert, that maybe you're playing too many games simultaneously online. You get the different tables mixed up on your screen. Instead of overlapping them to prevent confusion, you spread them around your screen and end up not being able to follow which bet and raise went where.

Now ask yourself: How the hell does anyone know what anyone else is doing at the same time he's playing online poker?

Next you hear the proclamations that so many more hands are played online per hour and you can't avoid any of them because your hands twitch involuntarily on the mouse and activate your calling when you should be folding. You also have no peer pressure to play properly and you can't read tells from any of these unseen peers, anyway, which makes you a bigger legitimate loser. Then you're in games that get so loose you're eventually forced to go on what's been coined "online tilt," to which my response is that the guys coining a phrase that bad should stick to watching *Tilt* on Challenge TV and forget telling everyone who plays online what *they* don't know about playing online. Especially when it comes to cheating.

This ridiculous myriad of observations as to why players think they're being cheated online when in fact they aren't has the cumulative effect of making us paranoid, which, of course, drives us to play differently and forces us into detrimental strategy adjustments because we constantly fear the worst, even though we're constantly being told no one is cheating us online.

Now listen closely, and then read closely. I, Richard Marcus, am going to stake my name and reputation on the pure and simple fact that online cheating by online players is not just prevalent but epidemic. If it isn't, then my reputation as the world's all-time greatest casino cheater is a crock of shit. Well, heck, maybe I really am only second best. But that will not stop me from telling you what's going on out there in Cyber Land, UK and World.

Okay, I've finally got you champing on the bit. You want to know how they do it to you, how they cheat you out of your money without even having the guts to show their faces. No problem. I'll explain every cheating method I know of. By the time I'm done, you should be your own cyber-sleuth and informed enough to protect your ass online.

Online cheating methods

Collusion

As it is in brick and mortar cardrooms, collusion is the most common form of cheating in online poker. The very nature of Internet gambling, by which each gambler can comfortably hide inside the dark void of technology, breeds the rampant strains of collusion that spread through its murky world.

In online poker, deceitful team-play is usually perpetrated by multiple colluders who pool their brainpower and electronic wizardry to take control of the games. These gangs of dishonest geeks get along so loftily that they flock to the honey like birds of a feather. What I'm saying is that online you can run into any number of cyber-colluders right up to the maximum seats at the table. I'm not saying you'll find 10 colluders in a 10-handed game, although I guess such an occurrence would be possible if they were just practicing in the confines of an online scrimmage. It can get so spidery that sometimes it's a double-dealing operation where one player thinks he's working in collusion with another, but the other is really working in collusion with yet another against him. Talk about duplicity, maybe that's why they call it "the web." Online gambling can become the web of deception.

Anything goes in online collusion. You could actually have one five-man team of colluders battling it out on the same table with another five-man team of colluders, with neither team knowing the other team is a team. But for you honest players, the worst-case scenario on the Internet would be to run into a large team of colluders cheating only you. If you ever have the misfortune of colliding with a full table of colluders where you're the odd man out, I can only ask the heavens to bestow on you a royal flush on the flop while everyone else at the table makes quads at the river.

How do these colluders operate so swiftly when the security departments of online poker sites say they can't?

It's all in the hardware and it's all in the software. Two players can reveal their hole cards to each other via an instrument as simple as a telephone. Or they could use Instant Messenger. Provided they're good enough players and get you squeezed between them on the screen, they will wear you down—slowly, but faster than it happens at the live poker table. Naturally the strategy colluders use for playing the hands is nearly identical to that used in public cardrooms, though there are some adjustments due to the relative fact that online games, regardless of what the cheating *denialists* say, tend to be tighter than live games.

When these collusion teams get bigger and spread out to more than a single online table, they need to network better and therefore use Instant Messenger with multi-PCs and multi-accounts, even multi-Internet providers (IPs). The beauty of it is that one person all by his lonesome can work his own collusion scam by playing multiple hands at the same table. That's where the multi-IPs come in. Or to reverse that hypothetical situation, you might run into a game where every player at the table apart from you is actually sitting in the same row in the same Internet café. And you can bet your sweet ass they'd be having a whale of time laughing *their* asses off as they maneuver your money from your account to theirs.

I can tell you that online collusion teams do not bother working low-limit tables. If your Internet poker gig is $3–6 or $5–10 you can skip the next few paragraphs on collusion because it doesn't affect your games. You'll find the bulk of colluders in $10–20 games on up.

Most of these teams are very adept; they have to be. Contrary to what you might believe, it is much harder for these teams to avoid detection than in live poker games, in spite of the facts their members are unseen and cannot be caught signalling hands among one another by way of chip positioning and other physical gestures. The reason for this is that everyone else involved in the game, from the honest players to the online managers, is equipped with computers as well. Therefore, with programs such as *Poker Tracker*, players can keep track of all the hands played in the game, not only their own but those of everyone at the table. Then whenever they like, they can review and analyze the data to see if anything strikes them as suspicious. For example, if the report showed that two or three players were repeatedly raising one another, that data might mean some whipsawing was going on, especially if you notice that an odd player was often dropping out or losing on the river.

But the greatest threat to colluders is the software used by the sites themselves to monitor the games. They have the option of being able to go back and scrutinize everyone's hole cards if they deem certain actions for a hand worthy of investigation. For example, if a player who had put several raises and re-raises into a pot and then folded was discovered to have been holding 7-3 offsuit, the site would most definitely flag his action. Then on further monitoring, if the same player is caught raising and re-raising with another stiff, and with the same competing player or players in the pot, the site could at that moment conclude that a collusion ring is on its table and take immediate action against it.

Another telltale sign of collusion is the early folding of a strong hand before the flop. If on reviewing a hand, a site's security finds that a player holding a pair of kings folded while another player held a pair of aces, it might also take punitive action against both players.

When going up against this kind of scrutiny, colluders must be extremely careful. If conclusive evidence is found indicating collusion, the guilty parties might very well find themselves barred from the site. Furthermore, in blatant cases with concrete proof, those barred might find themselves with the added problem of having their accounts frozen.

Most online cardrooms claim to possess state of the art software that enables them to automatically pinpoint various suspicious activities among its clientele. One of the things spied on is unusually high win-rates. If a player or group of players often seen at the same table is consistently winning significant amounts of money, they may find themselves the subject of an investigation. Another of the undercover ploys used by many sites is tracking IP addresses with historical playing patterns. If certain players are found to historically play at the same table, then their hand-histories are studied to determine if there's evidence of collusion teams. The sites claim they have developed a whole new battery of automated features to protect its client base from collusion but have not revealed was it is.

I do agree that, if used optimally, the internal security-system software installed by the online sites is effective. I don't, however, believe that the real professional colluding teams are stopped by it. They may be slowed in certain instances, but as long as they follow the cardinal rules about not being too greedy and not working in adverse conditions, they will outfox online security more often than not.

Peter, another ex-casino-cheating associate of mine who got very much involved in online poker collusion, told me how he avoids detection problems, and then on the other hand told me what honest players can do to avoid running into people like him on the Internet.

The easiest place for colluders to get caught, he explained, is in short-handed games. That's because the sites know how profitable short-handed games are for organized cheaters. Firstly, you have more pots, each of which takes less time. Then you have a greater ratio of colluders to victims. If, for example, a three-man collusion team is ganged up on a single player with the rest of the table seats empty, the lone player has absolutely no shot of a profitable outcome. About the only way he could come off that table unscathed is to pick up pocket aces or flop nut flushes every hand, and even then he wouldn't win much. It's just exponentially more difficult to win when three or more players are crookedly lined up against you.

But in spite of this, collusion teams must often forego these favorable situations. They know that short-handed games are often monitored to flush them out. If they do hit these games, they must strike quickly and then move on to another site.

A key element to collusion teams for the protection of their operation is the constant switching of IP addresses. The same way people should periodically change their passwords for their e-mail accounts, colluders must change their IP's, albeit more frequently if they're making the online poker-cheating business their full-time occupation. In addition, they need to change everything pertinent to their online poker room accounts: surnames, bank accounts, credit cards, e-mail addresses, even real home addresses. Naturally I wondered how anybody could do all that. E-mail addresses and home addresses could be changed easily enough, but how does one change his surname and then open new bank and credit card accounts under the new name?

I was not prepared for the response I got. Peter looked at me with a twinkle in his eye and asked, "Did you ever hear of identity theft?"

It hit me. Of course these computer hackers surfing the online cardrooms were capable of pilfering a few IDs along the way. So all they had to do was keep signing into the Internet poker sites with totally new credentials: new name, bank account, credit card, and so on. Even when barred from an online cardroom, they could log right back on to the same site as someone else and play at the very same table on which their collusive activity had been detected. Talking about the "nuts!" This was ingenious, as it was outrageous. No matter what kind of security software was being used by the sites, no way they could keep up with online poker cheaters who were identity thieves to boot.

Can one person create a whole table of players against you?

Yes. Suppose he has nine computers in one room and uses one local connection to the Internet. Then he uses eight modems to call long distance dial-up accounts located in eight different areas of the country. He then creates nine different poker accounts under nine different names and has funds coming from nine different bank accounts in those areas where the dial-up accounts are located. The reason for different dial-up accounts is that they are given unique IP addresses, so the online site will see they are located in nine different areas. Even if the sites have detection software and see these players repeatedly at the same table, the master "self-colluder" can create dozens of more accounts and use them interchangeably to make it all appear random.

And you know what? He doesn't even need the nine computers! All he needs is one running VMware, which allows one running virtual machine to be paused, copied to other physical computers, and unpaused to resume execution exactly where it left off. In short, one physical computer runs numerous operating systems simultaneously.

Poker Devil

Back in the summer of 2002, a hacker-group of the slightly more honest variety began work on developing what they called the Scoop Monster program. They designed it to tell its users the precise odds of winning a current hand, and then advise them exactly how to proceed. To take it one step further, the hackers improved Scoop Monster so that it could be set to automatically play the hand for you. With that final product they were convinced that its users would be playing with a 4% advantage over the most skilled players online, one of the reasons being that Scoop Monster could never make a mistake or oversight, never misplay a hand.

The group sold several hundred of its software packets to dedicated online player-cheaters. These people launched an all-out Internet assault with their new babies. But a funny thing happened. According to conversations in poker chat rooms, there was a flaw in Scoop Monster's "autoplay" features. Nobody could really put his finger on it, but the end result for everyone using it seemed to be that it just didn't play well enough to win. Those who'd invested in it began to lose confidence, eventually to the point of letting it fall to the wayside, where it lost touch with the poker underground.

But the poker sites had been very disturbed by these experiments. Even though it appeared doubtful that crooked players could make worthwhile profits using even the latest version of the software, security at the Internet poker rooms grew very concerned and saw Scoop Monster as a latent threat to the Internet poker business, especially if the hackers worked out the kinks in the program. After all, the entire online poker business hinges on the concept of real players competing against one another. They certainly don't want it turned into the likes of chess and backgammon-playing against a computer.

Eventually, the poker sites announced that they had made improvements to their software which prevented players from using Scoop Monster, and when the veracity of that declaration was undermined, they decreed that anyone caught using it would have their online accounts terminated. At the end, these threats did work in the sites' favor, for a short time later Scoop Monster was taken off the market.

But it didn't end there. A year and a half later, in early 2004, another group of computer geeks wrote a program much stronger than the Scoop Monster it was based on. They called it Poker Devil. The kinks in the autoplay function were ironed out, and over the course of millions of hands it proved flawless, attaining that 4% edge its users sought so fervently.

This time, the threesome of geeks who wrote it did not put it up for sale on the mass market. They decided that rather than flood the Internet with their device, which would surely lead to overexposure and quicker countermeasures by the sites, they would form their own team and just keep the millions of online suckers for themselves. With a 4% edge and countless hours of play, the geeks had the foresight to recognize the vast potential of poker riches on the Internet. They set off on the cyber yellow brick road to riches.

As of today, the underground Poker Devil team is very healthy and has grown to a few hundred members. It is run as a large syndicate by the original three geeks. They function like an intricate actuarial firm, assigning numbers, times and hours of play among the four or five "branches" of the entity. They spread their play across the major sites and avoid each other's territory the same way that one Mafia group avoids the turf of another.

Poker robots

As we move into the second half of the new millennium's first decade, new online software is emerging that is sending Poker Devil back to hell. These new programs are outright poker robots. They do it all. You log in to your chosen site and the "bot" takes over. It's not just autoplay; it's *total* play. The bot determines what game you should play in relation to the size of your bankroll. It chooses the particular table for that game, based on the action and speed it desires. It plays your hands, then tells you when to quit and either find another table or go to bed. In short, you don't even need a brain to operate a poker bot. Heck, you can go to sleep, get laid, be laid or do whatever else you like while your bot goes online to fetch your poker winnings.

The end result is even better than the 4% edge you had with Poker Devil. I imagine that in the near future your bot may begin playing online while you're soaking up the sun on some faraway beach, and "he" won't even tell you he's playing. Let's just hope he's more honest than you and gives you the cut of his winnings you're entitled to.

Sounds terrifying, but you may be wondering how bots can use facets of poker other than probability and statistics to their advantage. After all, they can't read people's minds and process tells. Or can they?

The truth of the matter is they can do both. Bots are now equipped with artificial intelligence. The brains behind these bot programs have left nothing foreign to their realm. Today's bots even have personality. They can annoy you; they can assuage you, all in their style of play. One of the most powerful bots known to exist is called a "vex bot." This because it actually has the ability to *force* its opponents on tilt. But how does a vex bot adjust to playing against human beings, who have cornered the deception market and use that trade to outwit any innocent computer?

Well, consider this fact: The patterns poker players exhibit do change according to their strategies but they also remain the same for a given period of time.

Players shift their strategies either voluntarily or involuntarily. An example of a calculated shift would be when a tight player decides to play loose and calls more bets before the flop, especially from early position. This will in turn get that player more action when he's doing the betting with a strong hand. This type of play may continue for a length of time, but the tight player by nature eventually goes back to tight play.

The same theory holds true for naturally loose players when they elect to tighten up. At certain times in the game, they might want the opposition to believe they're tight players. By succeeding, the loose player posing as a tight one will have more success bluffing, because the table will put him on a good hand when he comes over the top with a raise.

Involuntary shifts in play arise most often when players go on tilt. That's when they lose their marbles and play in alternating bouts of passivity and aggression. It's the kind of pattern most difficult to chart.

So how would a computer do it?

Firstly, it reduces poker to its most basic components. It treats each player at the table apart from itself as a heads-up opponent. In that approach it is able to read each opponent's play and develop a strategy tailor-made for heads-up play against him.

Even when the bot is not involved in a pot, it never stops collecting data on the players conducting the action. After a given number of hands, the bot will actually recognize changes in each player's pattern that suggest either voluntary strategy or uncontrolled recklessness, the latter being the case when players go on tilt. The whole concept is that the bot does not need to see its opponents. It does not need to read tells. The proof in the pudding is that all players, even in live games, can never escape their pattern of play *while* they're playing it.

Site bots

Do the online sites have their own bots?
Would they use them to play against you?

Well, in a sense, sites already have them playing against you. It's no secret that bots are used to fill up play-money tables on sites. They claim that it's strictly a service for new players who want to practice playing online poker before venturing into the real-money games. And it is. People can play 24 hours a day on the play-money tables. In the long run, this service earns millions for the sites because nearly 100% of the play-money players graduate into real cash games. The sites claim that their bots have no advantage whatsoever against good human players. After all, what good would it do them to drop winning bots into their play-money games?

But something the sites don't mention: their bots can be programmed to be lesser than average players. Why? Because if the play-money players beat the games and come to believe they're good players themselves, the sites will have them upping the ante to real cash action quicker than you can say "buy-in."

Are there site bots in real-money games?

It has been suggested that the sites using props in real games may have had bots occupying their seats. If that were the case, it would be quite advantageous for the sites: the bots would draw players to otherwise short-handed games and at the same time earn money for the sites. In effect, it would be as though the site's revenue were increased by 1 or 2%, depending on the action.

I do not think bots are currently in action on the side of the sites, although I'm sure they were during the first few years of Internet poker. I am also of the opinion that their "start-up" performance was of a high enough quality that in their retirement the bots should be elected to the Online Poker Hall of Fame.

A final word about player bots: Let's just hope that in the cybergaming future we won't bear witness to online games where everyone is playing with a bot. Such a happening would create kind of a "Future Shock" scenario in which the online game would be nothing more than a circus of computers playing against computers, and it might be so evenly distributed that not one of the computers would ever have a reason to get up from the table.

Can the sites detect player bots?

The answer to this question is yes and no. Commercial bots that are not customized can be detected by sites' security software searching for certain patterns. For example, if a player sits at a table without leaving for a week and automatically posts blinds every hand, that would be an obvious sign of a commercial bot at work. Another suspicious one is when a player never responds to other players' attempts at conversation, although the silence in itself means little as many legitimate players do not "chat."

Today's sophisticated customized bots are created to camouflage themselves better than an army squad in a jungle. They not only know how to change seats, tables and even sites on their own, they can also alter playing patterns (tight versus aggressive), bluff intermittently, and even sport mouse drivers with smart-moving devices for delays and clicking so that a site could never know that something non-human is controlling the mouse.

Peeker

One morning in early 2004, while I was resting up after a ski vacation in the Swiss Alps, my buddy Peter telephoned me with this invite: "Richard, remember how you were asking me all those questions about cheating the online poker games? Well, come on over. I've got something to show you. It's a pleasant surprise. You should get a kick out of it."

I knew I would indeed. Peter and I went way back and we trusted each other implicitly. If he had something to show me on the cutting edge of cheating, he could do so without worrying it would go beyond me.

When I got to his house, I saw that the surprise he had in mind was not only pleasant; it was overwhelming. In his "study" he had a bank of computer monitors that looked like that of VCRs in casino surveillance rooms. The hard drives, with their platoons of coiled wires snaking up to the backs of the raised monitors, sat on the floor. I also noticed he had no fewer than 10 phone lines in the room. I remembered Peter telling me that he worked with a collusion team whose 50 members were scattered on five continents and spoke twice that many languages. I wondered if the phones were necessary only for duping the online sites into believing that 10 different players were at their tables when in fact there was only one who was armed with 10 computers. Or perhaps Peter liked conducting real simultaneous phone conversations with his colluding buddies as well.

My eyes came back to the monitors. Peter had multiple online games going on the screens. I counted four. One of the screens was turned off.

Up to that point in time I had only dabbled in online poker. I wasn't much of a legitimate gambler any more (to be one with my knowledge would be like a drug dealer getting high on his own supply), and even though I had participated in poker scams the thought of online cheating never intrigued me—until that day.

I recognized the familiar graphics of online games in progress: the players gathered around the table; their face-down cards and chips in front of them; the big white cards on board in the middle of the table. Peter was incessantly clicking four different mice as he played his hands in each game, all on different sites.

"Whom are you colluding with?" I asked, pointing at no particular screen.

He gave me a snickering laugh. "I don't bother with the

collusion any more."

That struck me as odd, but at the same time I thought perhaps I knew why. But I asked, anyway. "No more collusion?"

"Here, I'll show you why."

Peter's fingers glided over the mouse and he began clicking. The fifth screen came to life. He logged in at yet another online poker site, double-clicked to select a $20–40 hold'em table and then again to select a seat. Next he bought in for $800 in chips and promptly posted the big blind.

"No use waiting for the button to go around," he chirped, then instructed me to pay special attention to this screen only.

I watched the deal. It happened like any other deal I'd seen on Internet poker. The table was now full and each player had his two face-down cards in front of him.

"Don't piss in your pants when you see this," Peter preened, then jokingly added, "And don't tell anyone what you saw." He then made a series of mouse movements and clicks. After my brain took the second it needed to process the information it received from my eyes, I didn't piss in my pants. But I nearly shit a brick!

Suddenly those hole cards were not in the hole any more! Yes, that's what I said. Each player's two face-down cards were now bigger and face up and staring me in the face. I couldn't believe it. And, believe me, in my day not only have I seen quite a few amazing cheating tricks, I invented a few myself.

"How the hell did you do that?" I asked with such incredulity that Peter had to chuckle. He chuckled even more when I asked him if this was only a play-money game.

"I guess I never told you about David Woo."

"David who?"

"Woo."

"Who's he?"

"He's the guy who broke into this poker site's server and bypassed the code."

"What code?" I was not very computer literate. Neither was Peter but he'd obviously been a quick learner.

"It's called the encryption algorithm. That's the part of the website's software that protects everyone's hand and prevents anyone from seeing other people's hole cards."

"That's fucking amazing!" I exclaimed after whistling.

"That's online poker reality," Peter said as calmly as if we'd been talking about how to "google" a celebrity. He let me know that among the privileged who possessed it, the software was called Peeker.

"How many people can do this?" I wasn't sure that I wasn't thinking I wanted to add my name to that rarefied list.

"Well, for starters, I'd tell you only those with the software to break the code for the encryption algorithm. If you can't make those programs yourself, you have to buy them. They're expensive."

I already had knowledge about sophisticated computerized equipment used to cheat at gambling. Just after my book *The Great Casino Heist* was published in Great Britain, I received an e-mail on my website from a guy named Chris who wanted to recruit me to join his roulette-cheating team. I was intrigued by his e-mail and curious about the high-tech equipment he said he possessed, which he claimed could very accurately predict the six-number section of the spinning wheel that roulette balls would land on. It turned out he was talking about computers whose scanners told you where the ball would land before it made its final descent into the grooves on the wheel.

Being the kind of guy who's always been interested in new casino-cheating innovations, I flew over to London and met Chris. He showed me his equipment, and with his teammate gave me an actual demonstration of how it worked in two London casinos. As a matter of fact, it worked quite well and they made a few scores. Chris told me they had paid £10,000 for the computer and transmitter, and that for double the price they could purchase a laser capable of pinpointing the exact number on which a roulette ball in midspin would land, better than 30% of the time. Were that true, the profits for those using the laser would be enormous, because the true odds of hitting a number straight up on a single spin are 37 to 1 on American wheels and 36 to 1 on their English counterparts.

I was pretty much fascinated by their roulette scam, but being retired (at least for the moment as I am now) I wasn't impressed to the point of coming out of retirement.

I asked Peter if he had a rough idea as to how many people around the world cheat online poker with that kind of software and how long could they go on using it before the sites got wise and major criminal arrests took place.

Peter explained that it was impossible to estimate the number of people who had both the money and desire required to purchase the software. He knew lots of people interested in making money by cheating at online poker, but putting up 30 grand to buy Peeker was very exclusive. He also enlightened me that Peeker was available only on the "white market," which meant that not just anyone could buy, even if he had the money. The inventors of the software actually had the integrity to keep their product out of the hands of those who by misuse would shorten the life of its productivity. Peeker could not be copied. Something that good was not about to become available as a freebie.

Peter was as informed about the subject as anyone fucking with it had to be. Like any other cheating device in gambling, the software that breached the poker sites' hidden code had a

finite life. One day it would be rendered useless by still another cybersphere technological development. That future
laser for roulette those British guys spoke to me about has already been rendered obsolete by the Eastern Europeans who
got caught using it in London's casinos. They may have pock-
eted a few million during its life, but as for future beneficiar-
ies of that sort of equipment—forget it. Pretty soon you won't
be able to give lasers away.

Same theory applied to Peter's software, though for the
moment I watched in awe as he clicked his mouse like a pian-
ist stuck on the winning key. He was able to play perfect
poker and didn't have to worry about his play being discovered by some security team going back over the pots he won
and folded on. I did ask him if he ever called with losing
hands. He responded that it was necessary from time to time
just to keep up the appearance of *not* being able to see his opponents' hole cards. While watching more chips come his
way on the screen, Peter let me know that the advantage of
seeing everyone's hole cards (which also allowed him to cal-
culate more accurately the outs he had on any given hand)
was so strong it was to all intents and purposes "off the
scale."

The most incredible hand I viewed that day was one that
Peter lost. He had abandoned the other games he'd been playing and was now solely devoted to a huge Omaha hi pot-limit
game with blinds of $50 and a $100, according to him the biggest poker game offered online. It was on a site frequented by
British players who loved the game.

One player at the table used the handle "True Brit" while
another chose "True Grit." I don't know if these players knew
each other, but I doubted they were in collusion, because using such similar monikers would be pretty damn stupid if
they were. In any event, Peter said he'd never seen either

name playing Internet poker (which doesn't mean they hadn't played under different handles), nor did he care if they were in collusion against him.

"I can see their fucking hole cards," he said with finality.

That hand, True Brit in fourth position was dealt A♦-J♦-3♥-3♣; Peter in sixth position was dealt A♠-A♣-K♠-K♥, and True Grit on the button received 7♠-7♦-2♠-2♥. True Brit, although unseen, must have smiled at his suited high-diamonds next to his small pair. He raised the big blind $100. Peter, with his monster pairs of aces and kings, and the added luxury of seeing everyone's hole cards, slowplayed by simply calling. True Grit, who would have undoubtedly folded had Peter re-raised or had he not been on the button, limped in with his two weak pairs. The rest of the table folded.

The flop came K♦-3♦-2♣. It was a big flop for each of the three players. Though for True Brit it was a true bonanza. Not only did he flop the nut flush draw but also trip-3s. Peter flopped trip kings and True Grit flopped trip deuces.

A huge pot loomed in the air.

True Brit bet $200. Peter, who of course saw that his hand was best on the flop, did not hesitate to call but balked at raising. If the board paired with another diamond on the turn or river, he'd have a monster winner and probable three-way action. He didn't want to force the opposition out of the pot. By the same token, True Grit certainly did not want to throw away his trips, low as they may be, so he called.

The turn came A♥.

Peter let out a whistle and said in a wowed tone, "I'm sitting here with trip-aces and trip-kings. I feel like I'm the Queen of Sheba." I watched the screen intently. I sensed the huge pot developing.

Still holding the nut flush draw and trip-3s, True Brit decided it was time to make his move, probably figuring that if the board paired on the river he might be in trouble. He bet out $500. Peter circled the mouse around the call and raise boxes, seemingly indecisive about raising. His index finger momentarily wavered with the mouse in the raise box but he ended up only calling.

The unexpected big move on the turn came from True Grit. Out of nowhere he bet the pot, $2,350. He probably put True Brit on the flush draw, ignorant that True Brit's latent second best hand already had his beat. Likewise, True Grit probably put Peter on a lesser value hand than he in fact had. In any event, True Grit's betting the pot was a huge move.

True Brit absolutely had to call. He actually had more outs than Peter, who had traced the hole cards discarded by the players who'd folded before the flop. Peter was able to ascertain that there were four diamonds in the remaining eight cards. And the case 3 was still in the deck. This meant that True Brit had an approximate 5 in 8 chance of drawing out to the best hand. So his clicking in the call box was an excellent play.

Clicking in the call box was also the right play for Peter. The pot-odds made his call a worthy one, even though he was an underdog in the hand. He knew he had no chance to finish with the best hand if the board paired; the case ace and king were already gone. But still, the odds on his money justified his call.

After Peter clicked his call, there was $9,400 in the pot.

I had known Peter for a long time. Never before had I seen him so worked up about a hand of poker—online or off. It was as if the cheating wasn't part of it any more. Only the juice of anticipating that river card mattered to him. Nothing else made a difference. That Peter's Peeker software was incapable of identifying cards before they were dealt seemed unimportant to him.

That river card was one of the most amazing Peter and I had ever seen. Yes, it was a diamond giving True Brit the nut flush, but he didn't need it any more because he also made a full house of 3s over deuces. But his full house followed his nut flush right into the toilet because that diamond on the river happened to be the *deuce* of diamonds. That deuce gave Peter the nut full house, aces over deuces, a monster hand.

But it was a monster *losing* hand because True Grit made quads! Four fucking deuces on the river. So at the end, the three hands were quad-2s, aces-full and 3s-full, and an alternate hand of ace-high flush.

Peter simply laughed as he mumbled, "Thank God for this Peeker program."

I could only guess how much cash it saved him, but it was no less than $9,400. Had Peter been playing on the square, he would have had to call at least one more pot-bet.

True Brit, ostensibly unsure how to play his hand, bet $1,000. Peter clicked in the fold box. Of course True Grit bet the pot, which was now $10,400. He had the nut-nut: four friggin' deuces. Poor True Brit, who lost a total of $14,650 after calling the last pot-bet. Peter only lost $3,250 and laughed it off as an experience he was glad to have paid for. I took that to mean he'd have his money back from that loss after playing a few more hands.

I did the math again in my head. If the Peeker software had saved Peter $9,400 on that hand alone, how much would it increase his earnings over the course of a year playing high-stakes online poker?

"That's why I gotta play as much as possible," he said. "Before the sites knock this software into oblivion." It was an ominous forethought, but to this day that has not happened. Peter is still playing with Peeker, and he's a very rich man who has never had his account frozen by an Internet poker room.

That day watching Peter clean up online with his Peeker software was perhaps the most educational experience of my professional cheating career. I watched with my own eyes as his opponents' hole cards lay face up on the screen. At one point I had thought that maybe he was playing a joke on me. Perhaps he'd just created a CD and played it for my amusement. But when he later showed me his activity reports from the sites and the monthly statements from his accounts, I could see that this was as far away from a joke as it was from Peter's offshore bank in the Caribbean.

So what would the sites be able to do *today* to stop this—besides waiting for its own programmers to develop software to protect the software already protecting the integrity of their games?

Peter's answer was simple: "Nothing."

And I understood. Sometimes scams (with or without equipment) are so good they cannot be countered. I once had one of my own. As seen on *The World's Greatest Gambling Scams* episode depicting my life as a casino cheat, I had developed a roulette "pinching" move that was called the greatest casino-cheating move of all-time by way of manipulating gambling chips. Both George Joseph, Las Vegas's number-one surveillance expert, and Andy Anderson, the most revered Griffin Investigations agent ever (who literally put hundreds of cheaters in jail over his career), attested to the greatness of my move. Anderson actually said—and I quote, "We never did come up with a way to stop it. Finally we just began refusing to pay it." The reasoning behind that decision was that a known cheater like myself could not go file identical complaints to the Gaming Control Board against every casino on the strip. By locking me out of payoffs they effectively stopped my move, if only for a time.

So Peter's code-cracking software would meet a similar demise, but who knew how much time that would take?

Don't think for a second that when this does happen, Peter and all his well-equipped online cheating peers will be out of business. Although the kind of software that allows you to read hole cards is probably the strongest program in existence (outside of one that would just let you steal the money without even playing), there are others being developed every day. I imagine that by the time you're reading this, a new software even more advanced than Peeker will be available—but for a very steep price.

Cheating in online tournaments

Is there cheating in online tournaments?

The occurrence of cheating in online tournaments tends to rival that of dishonest play on the sites' real-money games. Since the sites' security measures protecting the integrity of their tournaments do not differ from those safeguarding their real-money games, there would be no inclination by cheaters to cheat more or less in one form of online poker than the other. Decisions as to which segment of online play to attack reside solely in projected profitability for any given time or instance.

As collusion play is so rampant in the world's most renowned live poker tournaments, it is equally invasive throughout online competition. In fact, many of the major live-tournament-cheating syndicates save considerable amounts of money by using collusion tactics to win online tournaments offering seats to the WSOP and other prestigious live events in lieu of prize money.

The biggest advantage online poker tournament cheaters have over their brick and mortar counterparts is that they can use methods of cheating other than collusion. The most effective of these would of course be software that allows them to see opponents' hole cards or interfere with the integrity of the sites' RNGs and shuffling algorithms. To date we have not heard of a cheating scandal taking place in an online tournament, but if a site uncovered one, I doubt we'd hear about it.

Are there cheating teams that work both online and off?

Very few, and they are the cream of the crop. The one that I personally know of consists of two internationally known live tournament players, who are often seen on TV, and a close friend of my ex-cheating associate, Peter, who told me about this team the day he gave me the demonstration of his Peeker software. Peter called this select group of poker cheats the "A-Team," and said that their exploits would indeed be worthy of a TV series like the one of the same name starring George Peppard and Mr. T. They have captured many events, both at the WSOP and in the richest tournaments online.

But what Peter said that really reverberated in my brain was that one of the famous players on this cheating team is also a representative at a major online site.

Talking about getting the best of both worlds!

Lesser methods of online cheating

Not all online poker players with larcenous hearts and deceptive minds have either the means or know-how required to obtain the sophisticated cheating devices I have described. Many of these people must resort to whatever tactics are available to them. Although they are usually much less profitable, they still deserve mention if my coverage of online cheating is to be complete.

One low-level form of online cheating involves the abuse of the sites' "automatic all-in" feature. This added facet to online poker was created to resolve disputes caused by the Internet itself, problems that have nothing to do with the playing of poker but rather those related to Internet routing problems and personal computer crashes. When these breakdowns occur with a player in the middle of a hand, the site automatically puts that player all-in for money that has already been placed in the pot. The same measure is taken when a player simply does not act in the allotted time. The players remaining in the hand carry on by contesting a side pot.

The vast majority of these player stalls are unintentional. Usually it's an Internet connection problem or a plain oversight by the player. Maybe he went to the bathroom, forgot the pizza was in the oven or got interrupted by a phone call.

But sometimes these ordinary scenarios are not the case. In trying situations, dishonest players might choose to deliberately disconnect themselves from the site instead of having to deal with a difficult decision whether they should call a bet in a large pot. In some online cardrooms, if a player times out and is still connected to the game server, then his hand is automatically folded. In spite of this, it's still a matter for the site to decide whether the instance was intentional or accidental. Believe it or not, all-in abuse is cause for exclusion from poker sites. My advice to players suspecting others of this infraction is to promptly report the incidents to the site for investigation.

Also beware of the advance-action check-boxes that are now a standard feature of all the sites. Overall they speed up the game and allow players the liberty to make decisions before it comes around to their turn, but cagey opponents can take advantage of clues that your use of check-boxes may provide.

For example, let's say you have a monster hand before the flop. You decide to raise no matter what and click the advance box "raise any." But say the player before you raises while you get up to fetch a beer. You end up instantly re-raising because of your use of the advance-action "raise any" feature. That instantaneous action could tip off your opponents to the fact that you have the best hand and therefore cost you money when they drop out.

Some crafty players will simulate use of the "raise any" box by acting almost instantaneously when they are in late position and no one has yet entered the pot. This move is de-signed to steal the blinds by persuading the remaining play-ers that they would have raised in any circumstance.

Many different tells can be gleaned from the use of ad-vance-action check-boxes, therefore, I would suggest that you use them sparingly. They are best for "auto-posting" your blinds and mucking your bad hands when you have abso-lutely no intention of contesting a pot. If you insist on using this online feature more regularly, take advantage of the "random in-turn delay" option offered by most sites. This fea-ture allows you to vary your advance-action decisions, which camouflages your play because the software will insert a pause of random duration when it comes to your turn.

Another form of online poker cheating is misuse of the chat box provided by the sites. This is definitely the most amateurish form of Internet cheating I know of, but nonethe-less, at times it's effective. Usually it's committed by players who have just met at the game and have no real motive to cheat other than they feel like they've just made friends. What they'll do to help out a comrade is hint at what their hole cards are. To security people monitoring the sites, these hints sound more like blatant declarations such as "I have ace-king suited."

Another common form of illegal help via the chat box is when male players give their female counterparts tips on how to play hands. The motive here is always that these guys want to get laid, even if it's only a cyberfuck with an unseen partner! And I'm not saying that such flirtatious help only runs in one direction. Many skilled lady players sensing a male counterpart is both charming and in need of poker help gladly give it.

On the other end of this spectrum are those who try using the chat box to beat you. First, of course, they'll look for tells. Certain things you say online might coincide with whether you're bluffing or playing a solid hand. You may not be cognizant that just because you're unseen doesn't mean you're unreadable. There are players who need only to sense your tone of voice through your typing to beat you. They are very deft and clever, so watch out what you say and how often you say it. If not, when you type "lol," the laugh might be on you!

On the opposite side of the coin, watch out for those who are trying to throw you off by what they say and how they say it. In short, best is to talk, flirt and simply have a good time bullshitting while you're playing online. If another player's (or players') chat bothers you in any way, or sounds unnatural, break it off immediately. You've got nothing to gain by engaging in unpleasant or unwanted conversation, just as you don't in real life.

Lastly, be aware of the "shrinks" playing online poker while chatting away. These people will use any kind of psychological ploy to either upset your game or play in a way that gives them the advantage over you. At times they may abuse you verbally. Other times they may butter you up with false praise. A good rule of thumb I can pass on to you about the chat box is "don't place your trust in whom you can't see."

FAQs about online poker cheating

How can I protect myself from all forms of online poker cheating?

Well, besides my telling you to play Scrabble instead of online poker, you really can't. But I can give you some pointers to reduce the amount of time you expose yourself to online cheaters as well as the size of the chunk they bite out of your bankroll.

First of all, don't be paranoid about getting cheated. It's true that maybe 10% of all poker players, from live cardrooms to big tournaments to the Internet, are cheaters in some sense of the word. But you can reduce their numbers simply by avoiding them as much as possible.

Okay, let's go to the basics of online poker play. The first thing you must do is choose the site you want to play on. This is crucial because if you choose the wrong site, you won't even have to worry about getting cheated at poker. You'll just get robbed blind by the site! And I don't mean by way of crooked software fixing the deal against you, or by the installation of advantage-playing props in the empty chairs at your table.

I'm talking about online poker rooms going bust and out of business. Many of them have proven to be unscrupulous and left a trail of angry customers in their wake, mainly people who've never had their deposits returned to them. It's happened more often than you think.

These ripoffs are not always the result of fallen sites headed by thieving pricks. I will bring the case of Pokerspot to light. It launched with its own proprietary software in June 2000. Within less than a year it had built a client base of more than a thousand real-money players. But the site ran into serious problems when the payment provider it was using had its assets frozen by Barclays Bank because of "financial irregularities." Soon afterward the site stopped operating, and to this day has not managed to resolve its problems. Nearly half a million dollars belonging to Pokerspot's clients have never been returned to them.

Some sites have vanished without apparent reason, at least not legal, bank-related reasons. They tend to disappear like a bleep on your computer screen, with no server, no website, no support and absolutely no chance of its clients ever seeing their money again.

Other sites, although you won't find many of them admitting it, have been forced out of business because their software security codes got cracked. Early on in online gaming history, there were several successful teams of computer hackers that were able to break into systems and bug the software with programs enabling them to read the hole cards. (The Peeker software is much more complex than that of ancient hacking programs from the debutante era of Internet poker.) Many sites were forced into ruin when their reputations got muddied and clients lost all confidence of getting a fair game in their poker rooms. In the end it was those very clients who got screwed. Rarely did one of these victim-sites give a last breath of returning their money before going under.

In conclusion to selecting a site to play on, besides making sure you're dealing with an established one whose reputation is beyond reproach, don't forget that *no* site is a bank. Don't leave a great portion of your bankroll on deposit with sites and cash out as often as they will let you. If you follow these simple rules, you won't get hurt should the site disappear like a knight on a dog.

After determining at which site you would like to play and for what stakes, you must then decide which opponents you will play against. This is probably the single most important decision in online poker as far as anti-cheating is concerned. It is one aspect of the game that is controllable up to a significant point by the player. Obviously by identifying players frequenting the poker sites, you can follow their histories, and by evaluating the data determine if they might be parts of collusion teams.

For example, you want to play $10–20 hold'em. You log in to a large site and you see several games in progress. Viewing them, you notice three players at one table who you remember seeing at the same table a short while ago. Does this mean anything? Certainly. It means that there's an excellent chance they're a collusion team. If you see the same three, or even two of them at the same table a third time, you can take it to the bank that they're a collusion team.

Now let's say you've conducted an overview of several sites and found a table at which you'd like to play because you recognize none of the handles from previous action. You enter the game and begin play. It is of the utmost importance that you pay attention to your game if you want to pick up on cheating piranhas out to get you. When you're not involved in pots, instead of making telephone calls or running to the fridge, watch the action and take notes. Chart the hands that have multiple raises and re-raises between the same two, three or four players. If, by the end of your session, your information tells you that certain players were involved in an inordinate amount of duelling it out, especially with someone whipsawed between them, you can reasonably conclude that you've stumbled onto a heretofore unknown collusion team. Also remember that cheaters constantly change their handles. Jumping Judy whom you're playing against today might very well be Stand-Still Stanley who cheated your underwear off yesterday.

So what should you do about it? If you suspect certain players are teamed up against you, should you report it to the site and try getting the suspicious players barred? I would tell you not to bother. It's true that the sites encourage you to report any anomalies in the action that raise your concerns. They say that people tagged as colluders will become barred from the sites, and maybe even have their accounts frozen as the start of a litigation process. But I don't know how much of this is hype and how much of this is a real online Griffin Investigations Agency.

Always keep in the back of your mind that no matter how big online poker has become, it could be gone tomorrow, and these billion-dollar sites could be reduced to cyberspace backroom grind joints. This real possibility, which many powerful people in the US government are working around the clock to make reality, is also lurking in the minds of the people who run the sites. With such an overburdening threat of extinction hanging over their very existence, the online poker hierarchy is not going to worry so much about policing colluders, regardless how much they tell you that doing so is high up on their list of operational procedures.

Better you just keep your detective work to yourself. Each time you spot colluders and take note of them, you have more information to which you can refer the next time you go online to play poker. Simply put, serve as your own internal security. Don't depend on the sites' promises to protect you. In most cases, they would rather deny that collusion teams are running wild on their tables than deal with your complaints.

How can I assure myself that the sites' RNGs are truly random, and if I find they're not, what should I do?

My recommendation would be to go out and get yourself a good online poker program like Poker Tracker. These programs are able to monitor hand histories on the poker sites with a great amount of detail. What they do is create databases of games that occur on the site. Then they run through them to look for statistical inconsistencies. They search for unusual deviations in deck shuffles, draws and other details picked up by their trackers.

Let's use a particular outcome as an example of how this works. Remember I spoke of how flush draws and made flushes seemed excessive on some particular sites? Well, now we're actually going to run a simulated test to see if that's true.

Let's say you're in a hand and you have two suited spades in the hole. The probability of flopping four to the flush is around 11%. The probability of flopping the flush is a little less than .0085%. If you don't catch the flush on the flop, which contained two spades, then your probability of making the flush if you stay until the river is approximately 33%. In essence, the chance the board will have three to a suit-fall is close to 35%.

A good test sample would be 20,000 hands, which is no problem for your tracking software. Suppose that after the sampling your data tells you the following: suited hole cards flopped four to the flush 11.5% of the time; suited hole cards flopped the flush .009% of the time; suited hole cards completed the flush on the turn or river 33.5% of the time.

What should your analysis of this data conclude?

I'd say that only a slightly higher than random blip occurred, but not more than that. Looking at that feedback would not make me suspicious that the site is using preferential RNGs to distribute the cards.

Now let's say the sampling gives us these returns: suited hole cards flopped four to the flush 12.5% of the time; suited hole cards flopped the flush 1% of the time; suited hole cards completed the flush on the turn or river 36% of the time.

Now what would you think? Is this a little *too* much of an upward deviation?

Absolutely. If you saw numbers like these, you would have to conclude that the blip is very large and something is not kosher with the RNG. I would add, however, that this kind of deviation is not cheating you directly. It's only creating more action on flushes and therefore more dollars on the rake to the site. The effect of this on the overall body of players is that winners will win more money while losers lose more money.

There are, nonetheless, types of data sampling you can run to see if you are the *direct* victim of deviant RNGs or sophisticated cheaters. The most efficient would be to keep win–loss records against opponents with whom you find yourself at showdown. This would be similar to charting athletes' performances against individual teams. The results given from this kind of sampling are not as concrete for those derived in the "flush sample" above, but they can be useful in your evaluation of a site and its players.

Normally, over the course of 500 showdowns at which you are heads-up with another player, you should win around half of them. You can break this down further by assuming you would win around two-thirds of the pots when your opponent is calling you and one-third when you're calling him. You must also take into account the deviation in the breakdown of who's calling whom, but for the sake of this argument we assume that you call him half the time and vice-versa.

Let's next take this a step further and divide the 500 showdowns you're in by 10 players, so you're heads up with 10 different players 50 times each. Now we'll say that your results against them individually are as follows:

Against Player A:	You Win 26	Lose 24
Against Player B:	You Win 22	Lose 28
Against Player C:	You Win 25	Lose 25
Against Player D:	You Win 11	Lose 39
Against Player E:	You Win 30	Lose 20
Against Player F:	You Win 23	Lose 27
Against Player G:	You Win 15	Lose 35
Against Player H:	You Win 5	Lose 45
Against Player I:	You Win 28	Lose 22
Against Player J:	You Win 24	Lose 26

What do these results indicate? Let's break them down.

Against Players B, F and J, you lost within an acceptable deviation, given that their level of play is not significantly lower than yours. Against Players A, C, E and I, you either won more hands or broke out even (pot-amounts are not relevant in the sampling). By virtue of your not losing more than winning against these four opponents, you can dismiss them as non-suspicious players. After all, had they been colluding or cheating you in some other manner, their results are not very impressive and you'd be able to dismiss them as very bad cheaters, who do, by the way, exist in both online and live poker. If that's not the case, then you're one lucky bastard!

Which brings us to Players D, G and H. Against them you did not fare very well. In fact, they probably cheated you, at least according to the hypothesis that their level of play next to yours is not superior to the point where such huge deviations in the outcomes would have been reasonable.

Players D and G gave you a pretty good walloping. The numbers from the sample might suggest they're part of a collusion team against you, most definitely if the numbers had been compiled in instances with you and them at the same table, or together at different tables over a period of time.

Your record against Player H is very abnormal and should shoot warning flags in the form of missiles all over your computer screen. Losing 45 out of 50 hands to a player heads-up is indicative of something very strong working against you. In this instance, I am going to suggest that you're up in the face of a force that will rip your poker hands to shreds. It's got to be someone beating you to death with software enabling him to see your hole cards, for even the best poker bot could not post such annihilating winning numbers, not just against you but also against your mother who never plays anything but canasta.

If you want to detect colluders and cheaters without having to rely solely on samples of showdowns, just keep track of how many times you were raised and re-raised out of pots on the turn and river. Assign each time you were bumped out of a pot to the handles of players who raised and re-raised on that betting round. I guarantee that in doing this you will notice some pretty discernible patterns very quickly.

I can suggest one other way to find out if you're being cheated, either online or in live play. Just ask me directly.

That's right. My website is www.richardmarcusbooks.com. If you have a question about cheating, e-mail me and I promise to address it and get back to you. You will need to be as accurate as possible in supplying criteria for your situation. If you do that, I am very confident I'll be able to draw the right conclusion and send you back some sound advice.

What are the three most important precautions I can take in order to avoid becoming a victim to online casino colluders?

The first, of course, would be to not log on, ever. But in the assumption that you are not going to *never* log on, I would say the most important safeguard to protect yourself from the colluders is to look for games in which you recognize players against whom you've previously done well. If you spot a pair of players who have in the past beaten you, then maybe look for another game, even at slightly higher or lower limits. These players might be colluding against you. You're better off playing at unfamiliar limits than getting into a cheater's game at your regular limits. Be extra wary when you notice more than two players from a previous game in which you lost heavily, especially if an abnormally high percentage of your losing hands were to them.

The second protection device is to avoid short-handed games. The venom of collusion play is most deadly when a gang of snakes wraps around you and chokes off your hands. If you get involved against one of these teams, that mistake in conjunction with the speed of a short-handed game can send you so quickly to the cleaners it will make your head spin. You might also stay away from high–lowhigh–low split-pot games as they are preferred areas of prey for collusion teams.

The third thing you can do is keep good histories of all your online action. By doing this and then studying and analyzing your data, your cognitive powers will allow you to spot things that will sprout up red flags of danger. For example, if you play on sites whose hand-history features reveal the pocket cards of players who called and lost at showdown, you can figure out what they were doing in each hand and get a grip on different styles of play, some of which might arouse your suspicions. You can also do this when you are not involved in the showdown yourself; you can still see what the other players were going to war with.

Over time, you will notice who colluders might be, what times they tend to play, how often they make it to the same table, and so on. And besides using these records as an anti-cheating device, you'll find that by examining the data it will in many ways help your overall poker game.

Finally, you should know that online collusion will continue to thrive, regardless of what the sites say. They have over and over again reassured their clients and the rest of the world via Internet postings that they have measures, backup measures and backup-backup measures that can spot colluders in other galaxies. Naturally the sites are going to say this. The last thing they want is customers losing confidence in the integrity of their operations. Therefore, they must tell you whatever you need to hear, if only to keep you playing on line. Remember, there are no real controls forced on online cardrooms. In the brick and motor cardrooms of Nevada, for example, there is the Nevada Gaming Control Board Enforcement Division. It not only oversees the poker rooms but also makes sure everything the poker rooms announce to the public is true. The same type of real enforcement exists in all major gambling areas that offer live poker.

I am not saying that online poker cheating is so rampant that you need to delete the sites from your desktop. I am only advising you to play with caution. Cheating will proliferate online as it does in every facet of life pertaining to money. Just protect yourself.

Do online cheaters have a preferred time for stalking the sites?

Most of them do. Generally they favor playing off-peak hours because more hands get dealt, which increases their hourly win rate. For colluders, the off-peak hours are especially attractive in that they allow the team to gang up on the victim every hand. On hands where the victim folds early, the team can play out whatever they want very quickly: for example, having one guy bet out and his associate or associates folding. Then the next hand would start right up.

It's worth noting that cheaters keep track of peak and off-peak hours for the various sites just like regular players do.

Some sites are based in Europe, so the cheaters might congregate on the European online cardrooms while those operating from the Caribbean are in peak hours. But bear in mind that American-based players are barred from many European sites because of the legality issues shrouding Internet gambling in the United States. The result is that fewer online cheating syndicates are seen operating on the European sites than on the Caribbean ones, due to the fact that most of the well-organized cheat teams are American. Of course, these American teams take "online road trips" just like brick and mortar casino-cheaters do. Don't be surprised if you notice a bunch of nerdy-looking guys crossing the Mexican border at Tijuana in SUV's filled to the gills with laptops. You can bet 2 to 1 they're Internet cheating-geeks looking to hook into the European online cardrooms.

If you play on the major sites between 8pm and 11pm EST, you will be the safest from collusion cheaters because that's when the greatest percentage of players online, which is not a favorable condition for colluders. Other online cheaters using bots or hole-card-reading programs do not care about peak hours, so you might run into them at any time. Still, overall cheating online affects you less when you play peak hours.

Do online cheaters prefer certain sites?

Absolutely. Like in any business they prefer to be at the place where they can earn the most money in the quickest fashion. This usually occurs at the largest sites with the most active full and short-handed tables to choose from. But during certain hours, smaller sites may offer the biggest game being spread on the Internet. A good example of this would be finding a smaller site with a big Omaha pot-limit game going. Any pot or no-limit game with big enough blinds is going to glow in the dark for organized online cheaters.

Cheats will also look to play as much as possible on sites not known for aggressive security procedures. Although every major site claims to have sophisticated devices in place to identify collusion and other forms of cheating, this does not mean they are actively using them.

First and foremost, sites want their players to feel secure while gambling in their online games. Statements guaranteeing strong security are what build confidence in online players, but organized cheaters are very well informed. They know which sites have barred the most players suspected of cheating. They get first wind of the most demonstrative action taken by sites against cheaters: freezing of accounts. You can bet that when online cheaters hear about a particular site freezing clients' accounts, they will be quick to choose another site for their upcoming action.

Do online cheaters always look for higher-limit games? If I'm a small-limit player, can I put your book down now and just start enjoying myself playing poker online?

Well, before answering that, let me at least hope that you were enjoying my book before putting it down! But your question is valid. Online cheaters do search out the high-end games. After all, they can't make much money in a $2–4 game. But this doesn't mean you won't find cheating teams practicing at that level. And even if they haven't yet perfected their teamwork, they can still hurt you.

Is there really any instance of online cheating that warrants being reported to the site's security staff?

Yes, if you have provable evidence that one of the players using the chat box is trying to bird-dog your spouse while you're playing. Then maybe they can do something to thwart it. Besides that, I'd still say it's best to just move on to another table, or even another site, if you're leery about other players in the game. Gosh, there are so many sites nowadays that you should never experience more than one problematic episode of this nature in a 24-hour period.

If I suspect I'm being cheated by one of the various methods you've described and I notify the site, and then the site's security people find proof that I was indeed cheated, am I entitled to a refund of money lost to cheaters from the site?

Are you asking me if the casinos like to play Robin Hood? That is a good question—not about Robin Hood but whether you're entitled to recover money you were cheated out of. Unfortunately, it's not whether or not you're entitled to it that counts. It's whether you get it or not. Some sites have refunded losses to players who have been victims of what they called "proven" cheating. I cannot give you an exact set of requirements for proven cheating but would imagine that it's about 100% discretionary. In other words, if the site says you were cheated, then you were cheated. If you say you were cheated and the site says you weren't cheated, then it's tough titty on you. You can't go to the "Internet Gaming Commission" and demand a refund.

Policing of gaming on the Internet is rather limited. You can understand why. Computer cops have their hands full with terrorism and credit thieves. And please don't ask me if terrorists play poker. Okay, if you insist, I'll answer that they probably do. You want to take it *further!* Do they cheat? Yes, but no more than the most docile, friendly people who cheat you with smiles on their faces.

Is it possible that online sites use software that purposely helps novices win in play-money games so that they can hook them into their real-money games?

Damn right. It would be the easiest area for online sites to use crooked software. Since no real money is exchanging hands in play-money games, a site using software to "dump" worthless chips on you could never be accused of having actually ripped off anyone else in the game. I have spoken with many online veterans about their early days playing Internet poker. These are people who had no previous experience in live poker games before catching the bug. They actually learned the rules of poker at one of the sites. Nearly all of these players, practically 100 of them, conferred to me that they had much higher levels of success when playing in the fun games than they did once they hit the real-money tables. Many of these people professed regret at allowing themselves to have been "suckered in" to the for-keeps action.

Publicity departments of online sites have responded to this. Mainly they say that when playing poker with play money, people tend to play loosely and even foolishly and therefore experience both winning and losing variances far greater than in real-money games. Whether or not this is true, the players I've spoken with all claim to have played tight poker while learning the game, as they had already known the old poker adage that "loose play ends in a bad day."

Is there any relationship between the market share of a site and the percentage of its clientele prone to cheating?

This is a very difficult question to answer accurately. Many variables must be examined, such as type of cheating, number of cheaters and a site's internal security. Let's first look at two of the industry's largest sites: ParadisePoker and PartyPoker, each of which has been able to retain its position as a market leader with a huge client base. They both have constant action around the clock.

However, if you browse through the archives of online

poker forums, you will undoubtedly fall on more accusations of collusion and other forms of cheating for these two sites than any other. But does that mean more cheating actually goes on at ParadisePoker and PartyPoker than on smaller sites?

Absolutely not. In fact, the inverse is probably true.

Because these are the largest sites with the most tables and players, they will invariably have the most losers and the most losers who might feel they've been cheated. But let's not forget that these two sites will also consistently have the most winners. It's just a question of percentage. When you have comparatively large clienteles, you have large numbers of winners, losers and cheating victims. When examining the issue of cheating by player collusion, you might actually see less of it on the biggest sights because they have the lowest percentage of short-handed games.

I have previously put forth the argument that certain sites may be guilty of "juicing" their games to get more action. There's no question in my mind that this type of site-instigated cheating goes on, mainly because it is not direct cheating against any particular players; it's just to build bigger pots on the tables that attract more players to the sites. But again, there is no evidence that the bigger, better-known sites do this any more or less than start-up sites you've barely heard of. On the contrary, there is evidence that the games at the largest sites tend to be tighter than games at smaller ones, and tight games are far less likely to deal juiced hands.

Normally it's looser and split-pot games that attract the greatest number of cheaters. The distribution of loose games over the gamut of online poker tends to vary according to both sites and time of day. If you're trying to avoid very loose games, as I would suggest, you might want to monitor numerous games across the Internet daily or weekly, observing which sites tend to deal tighter, more trustworthy games. It's not a bad idea to take advantage of the note-taking and statistics functions that most sites offer. By doing that you will stay abreast of the shifting tendencies of tight and loose games as they change from site to site.

Is cheating more prevalent on sites that allow multiple-table players?

I have done a lot of research on this issue. The key to determining an increase or decrease of cheating with multiple-table players is to examine the motivation of players wanting to exercise their right to play at more than one table at a time. The first part of that puzzle is easily solvable. Everyone playing multiple tables thinks that by doing so they have some kind of edge, mainly increasing their win ratio over each unit of time played. But since we know that a player playing honestly in multiple games is subject to more mistakes and overall weaker play, due to the pressures of having to evaluate simultaneous situations and act quicker, we must question why players would subject themselves to that built-in fallibility.

It can be said that a strong player with a winning advantage of 2% in a single game might only have a 1.5% advantage in each of two simultaneous games, but that drop in effectiveness for each game would still give the player a combined 3% winning advantage. If the player is in two truly simultaneous games, he is not losing any time by playing the second game, therefore, that extra 1% advantage is concrete.

But that is only one explanation of player-motive for multiple table play. The other is, of course, cheating. As for collusion, its combined increased percentage advantage would fare about the same as honest play, since colluders are subject to the same errors and pressure situations as honest individual players.

If we were to parallel the example above, where a player normally having a 2% advantage at a single table would enjoy a combined 3% advantage in two games, we would see that a collusion team with a 5% advantage in a single game might raise that to 7.5% while in two simultaneous games. In either case, with honest or dishonest play, each additional simultaneous table played would increase overall advantage in diminishing increments up to a certain point, where the maximum number of multiple tables would be reached.

But when we talk about bots, you can throw those numbers out the window. Since these artificially intelligent monsters can play at a million tables just as easily as they can play at one, people employing them would certainly seek out sites allowing multiple-table play, especially those which allow more than two tables to be played simultaneously. If honest and regular collusion players gain a diminishing increase in returns with each additional table of simultaneous play, bots gain exponentially increasing returns for an infinite number of tables. But, comparatively speaking, there are much fewer functioning bots online than human colluders. In the future, I expect that to change.

What about all the big-name professional poker players who have linked up with the sites? Do they really believe in the product they're hawking or is it solely for their own publicity to increase their fortunes?

In the movie *The Sting*, Paul Newman makes the statement, "If you're sitting in a poker game and you look around the table and can't figure out who the sucker is, it's you."

Why am I answering that question with Newman's reasoning, which sounds pretty damn true to me? Because if you have to ask me it, you've proven you're the sucker.

Of course these pros who lend their names to online sites

are only in it for the money. Do you believe for a second that Michael Jordan eats Wheaties every morning? Or that Tiger Woods races against the tennis-playing Williams sisters to see who gets to the Gatorade bottle first?

As poker has become so big in recent years, endorsement contracts are going through the roof. Soon we'll see poker stars hawking everything from automobiles to the government's pitch for getting people to enlist in the Army. And it is not inconceivable that one day we will see the "Poker Super Bowl" on network TV, and I wouldn't be surprised if its ratings surpassed the NFL's Super Bowl. So believe me when I tell you that these poker pros care about the online sites they endorse about as much as you care which brand of shampoo you find in your hotel room's bathroom.

Bonus question:
Would you still consider cheating online, Richard Marcus?

I'll have to take the fifth.

CHAPTER SEVEN

CHEATING IN HOME GAMES

A lot of you who spend lots of time playing poker in public cardrooms or on the Internet may not realize that there are still poker players who play only at home or at their neighbors'. In fact, not only has home poker not fallen by the wayside but home games are more popular than ever.

From surveys conducted across the nation, we have learned that more bankers, lawyers, doctors and people on the unemployment line are playing home poker than ever before. And let's not forget the celebrities. Those you don't find mingling with top pros at the WSOP are highly likely to be playing poker at least once a week at some very impressive private address, with a mahogany poker table over which 100 million-dollar deals for the next few movies you'll see are discussed between pots. True, online poker and TV tournament poker may be responsible for the surge in home games, but many home players still do not play outside the comfort and familiarity of someone's house.

The very fact that home players come from all walks of life corresponds to the fact that home games will have their share of cheaters. Even at celebrity-studded home games in Beverly Hills you can find actors, writers, directors and producers who moonlight one night a week as poker cheats.

Do not doubt me; this is true. No class of people, regardless of their rung on the socio-economic ladder is above cheating. If that is untrue, then why do corporate honchos already worth tens of millions get caught all the time stealing hundreds of millions more? See what I'm getting at? So just remember that Tom from your bowling team or Louise from your neighborhood bakery may be taking you for a ride in your friendly Friday night poker game.

The first thing to know is that home poker games are the easiest poker venue at which to cheat. They are also the safest for the cheaters. After all, there is no sanctioned regulatory body to govern and watch over these games. It's only you and Bob, Dick, Harry and Shirley who can catch a cheat and then punish him. By punishing him, I mean either throw him out of the game or make him supply the doughnuts and coffee for each subsequent game over the next two years.

Which methods do home-game cheaters use? Well, just about all of them—and then some. I guess the only way they *wouldn't* be able to cheat is to use a bot against you. I reckon it would be rather difficult to have a robot sit between Harry and Shirley without Harry and Shirley, or someone else at the table, noticing that something's a bit strange with that certain player's demeanor.

The first time I ever cheated in a home game, I used one of the rankest moves of all time. And somehow I got away with it.

I was playing in my daily poker game, which was limited to 10 and 11 year-olds. The stakes were $2–4, by no means small potatoes for 10 and 11 year-olds. I wanted to buy a new baseball glove but I lacked the cash. So I decided that little Dewey Granger, a kid I didn't get along with, was going to help me pay for it.

In the mid 1960s, the game of choice for kids not yet at pu-
berty was five-card draw, high only. Lowball was as unheard
of as Texas hold'em. Our game was usually held in my friend
Steven Stevens' house. I truly loved his name, but the reason
we played at his house was because his mother was a degenerate gambler and the only parent who permitted us to play
under her roof. In fact, she even joined the game a few times
but stopped when her husband found out and berated her.

We were using a standard deck of Bee playing cards with
red backs. We didn't have any rules about changing decks
with blue-backed cards or anything like that. Normally one
deck of cards lasted for the duration of the game, maybe even
the next time we played as well. The deal rotated among the
players and each of us dealt his game of preference. That
preference was nearly always five-card-draw, although some
of the kids occasionally insisted on playing seven-card stud,
Chicago, baseball and seven-card bust.

Just before the deal got to me, we took a break. While
Dewey Granger and six other kids walked into the Stevens'
kitchen for some cookies and milk, I lagged behind, just long
enough to slip the red-backed Bee deck we'd been using in
my pocket and extract another red-backed Bee deck that had
been in my other pocket, which I placed in the middle of the
table. Naturally both decks were in about the same playing
shape. Then I quickly joined the gang in the kitchen so no one
would notice I had lingered at the poker table alone. Even at
that age nobody I knew trusted another human soul.

The eight of us back at the table, I began shuffling the
cards—falsely, of course. While everyone shot the breeze
waiting for the deal, I was able to make it appear I was mesh-
ing the two clumps of cards together. But just before they in-
terlocked, I broke them apart without losing the sound ac-
companying a normal shuffle. When the kid to my right cut

the cards, I just lumped the half-deck he cut right back on top without anyone noticing. Then everyone anted up and I dealt the cards.

I did not screw up. The four kings I had expected dutifully showed up in my hand. I took a quick gander at Dewey's face. I wanted to see if he was looking at me. If he was, then I might have chucked my kings right in the muck thinking he was on to me. But he wasn't. I could read in his eyes that he was staring at the hand I knew he was staring at: four 4s. I thought I detected the traces of a satisfied smile. He figured he would kick some ass this hand.

On the first round of betting, Dewey did not raise when the kid sitting next to him bet. He was slowplaying his big hand, trying to suck in the maximum amount of money into the pot before torpedoing everyone in the $4 betting-round after the draw. Well, I'd show the little prick!

Only one player folded before the draw, so there were seven of us left in the pot. Everyone up until Dewey drew three cards, forcing me to reshuffle the played cards because there weren't enough of them left to complete the draws. Dewey played it sly and took one, no doubt wishing to make everyone believe he was gunning for a straight or flush, or maybe a full house with two pair. Then the kid after him, Steven Stevens, showed an ace and drew four.

I decided to stay pat. Let everyone believe I already had a straight or a flush, and Dewey would surely think his four 4s destroyed my hand.

The first kid to act after the draw bet $4. Then a couple of folds to Dewey, who simply called, obviously hoping someone left in the pot had made a very strong hand lower than four 4s and would raise. He got his wish when Steven Stevens, who'd drawn four to his ace, raised the pot. I appreciated it even more than Dewey. While fixing up the deck, I'd only paid attention to the cards landing in Dewey's and my hands (we occupied the same seats every game), so Stevens' added action was a nice bonus.

At this point I let them have it. I came over the top with my $4 raise, making it $12 to go. The kid behind me folded as did the original better. When it came back to Dewey he naturally re-raised. Stevens called, and I adored it even more. The last thing I had expected in my debut as a poker cheat was to get three-way action in a killer pot I knew I'd win. I re-raised again, and so did Dewey. We played with unlimited raises, so this could keep going until money was run out of.

Then unbelievably Stevens re-raised again. I was thinking he probably made a monster aces-full boat. How lucky could I get? Not only would I buy my new baseball glove, I'd get a few bats and balls to go with it.

I re-raised, Dewey re-raised me and Stevens re-raised him. The bombardment of re-raises continued nonstop until Stevens ran out of money. But he was determined to re-raise yet again, and while pondering how to get more money to do so his mother walked into the room.

Right, you guessed it! Mrs. Stevens opened her purse and gave her son a $20 bill, but not without the admonishment that we should play five-card draw with limited raises.

Mrs. Stevens hung around to watch the outcome. I felt a little bad that she was about to see her son take such a beating and lose 20 bucks of her own money to boot. But the pleasure of seeing Granger go down more than made up for it. When Dewey finally did toss his cards face up on the table, he looked a little worried. I think we had all lost track of how much cash was in the pot, but there certainly was a sprawled heap of $1 and $5 bills on that table. And there was Mrs. Stevens' 20 right in the middle! Poor Dewey would have to get a second paper route to cover this loss.

I had the smile of the artful dodger when I flipped my four kings onto the table. Up until that point in my life, it was the best I'd ever felt. My four kings had me feeling like a real king. It was majestic. The sweetness of leaning into the table with my arms spread like a condor to rake in all that cash was nearly indescribable. Don't forget, I was between 10 and 11 years old.

Did you ever see one of those poker scenes in a movie, most likely an old western, where some expectant cowboy lunges across the table to scoop a winning pot of cash, and as he's sweeping it into his pile a grizzly hand suddenly grabs his wrist and orders him to "wait a minute!" And then of course another grizzly hand turns over the winning hand.

Well, Steven Stevens was just a 10-year-old kid and his hands were not grizzly, but one of his hands did stop me as I was sweeping the cash.

"Wait, Marcus!" he barked. "You lose!"

Of course it was a joke, right?

Well, if it was, it was on me.

"You have four kings," Stevens was saying as he laid down his hand like Paul Newman did in *The Sting*. "Read 'em and weep."

When I saw his hand I almost did weep. The little son of a bitch had four aces. Four aces! How did it happen?

Well, going back to the beginning of this story, I never did say that my first attempt at cheating a poker game was successful. I only said that I "got away with it." I mean I was 10 and a half years old, inexperienced, and I made the horrible mistake of not making sure that *everyone's* hand was accounted for in the crooked deck before dealing it. And of course I never did take into account the possibility of having to reshuffle. Maybe that's where I got burned.

I had to wait until the following baseball season to get the baseball glove. I guess the moral of the story is: if you're gonna cheat at home, only cheat at home. Not at your friend's house. I remember my grandfather saying something to that effect. He liked to say, "Don't ever gamble in anyone else's backyard." I always took that to mean I should beware of being cheated on someone else's turf, not becoming a victim of my own scam. But after that happened I wasn't so sure any more.

Relating that bungled experience to you covered one common form of cheating at home poker games: putting a "cooler" or stacked deck into the game. There are many other ways of cheating home games by "futzing" with the deck. The word means to manipulate or alter the deck in the game without replacing it. Sometimes the deck itself is the cheating instrument and doesn't have to be altered.

Because it already is.

Strippers

Never heard of strippers? Of course I'm not talking about those beautiful long-legged queens with perfect butts and big pearly breasts that shake and bounce as they dance around men whose only prayer is that they drop into their laps. No, I'm not talking about them. I'm talking about cards. That's right, playing cards.

They're called strippers.

Not as well known as marked decks, stripped (or shaved) decks can be quite effective when handled by even novice cheaters, the ones you're most likely to encounter in your friend's backyard poker game. A stripped deck looks like any ordinary deck of playing cards. The difference is that one side of the cards has been lightly shaved. Your eyes do not notice this minute change in shape.

But when you pull out any card from the deck and then reinsert it inversely, the slightly protruding edge from the unshaved side will tick your finger as it rubs along the deck. Thus you can slide that card right out of the deck, regardless of its position. If you invert a second card before "stripping," that card will slide out just as easily. In all other functions, the deck behaves as a normal one. It is important to note that inverted cards in quality stripped decks are only sensitive to the touch of cheaters feeling for them. The shaving has been so light that the vast majority of honest home players will not notice the gaffed cards as they are shifted about randomly during the course of the game.

It is extremely rare that cheaters attempt to slip stripped decks into play in public cardrooms. They are quite detectable to experienced poker room players and personnel. But in crooked home games strippers abound.

Say the host of your game is using stripped decks and everyone else at the table is unaware of their existence. All he need do is invert a few key cards (say the four aces) in the deck when he's dealing. Then at any time during the deal, he can slide them out as needed. The aces would not only serve the cheater as high cards but also as top cards for each suit, which would come in handy when the cheat is looking to make a flush.

This home-game cheater would require certain rudimentary skills to pull off the moves, but suffice it to say that stripped decks are so easily handled they make seasoned card mechanics out of raw tenderfoots in a matter of minutes!

My ex-partner, Pat, who worked with me to invent the famed Savannah casino-cheating move, grew up cheating the poker players of his village with stripped decks. He told me stories about the village's summer clambakes where it wasn't only the clams getting stripped. He said he'd been caught once, or rather that one time someone noticed the ridge of a card sticking out, but the person was so naïve that when Pat told him it was most likely a manufacturer's defect, the victim was content to toss out the deck and let Pat remove another from its wrapping. Of course that deck was stripped too.

Stripped decks are abundant in novelty shops just about anywhere. They are not promoted as cheating devices but rather as tools of card trickery. Anyone can get them. So be careful not to be the victim of this kind of card trickery in your friendly poker game.

To make sure you don't, just perform this simple test on any deck of cards entered into play: Cut the deck in half and invert one of the halves. Then shuffle the two halves into a single pack. Take the full deck and grip it firmly in a position you're comfortable with, vertically or horizontally. Wrap your fingers around all four edges. Now simply slide your fingers along the edges as you continue holding the deck tightly. If the complete perimeter of the deck is absolutely smooth, then it has not been shaved. However, if you notice that any part of an edge is not entirely smooth, you're probably feeling up a stripper, and she ain't as good-looking as the one dancing on top of the bar!

Card mechanics

I know just about all of you have already heard of card mechanics. They're the oily little creatures who often don't deal you the cards they're supposed to, or don't flop, turn and "river" the cards lying on top of the deck. Again, this cheating technique is not something seen very often in public cardrooms but it does happen. In your home games, however, watch out!

First try and spot the "peek." The peek is part of the "peek and deal" technique used by card mechanics. Just because the best of them are capable of sliding back the top card, pulling out the second and dealing it without causing as much as a rasp, does not mean they can cheat you with these talents. In order to make the talent of dealing seconds profitable, the mechanic must first know which card is at the top of his deck. Then by evaluating that card, he can choose to either deal it off normally from the top of the deck or slide it back and deal the second card in his deck.

The mechanic performs the peek by slightly squeezing the deck with enough pressure so that the resulting crease in the top card allows its left pip to flash into his view for an instant. A skilled card mechanic is very difficult to spot. It's highly unlikely that a bunch of accountants or TV actresses would be able to flush one out. So remember this: Dick the janitor or Billy, the guy who changes the bottles on the water cooler, might be the slick dude at the company poker game dealing you seconds and robbing your money.

Marked cards

I have already spoken extensively on the subject of marking cards, but those pages were in relation to very sophisticated equipment used by professional cheating teams. For purposes of home games, we shall assume that none of your social drinking and smoking buddies are into that kind of stuff. The methods home cheaters use to mark cards are pretty rudimentary. Their goal is to put a little crease here, a crimp there, a fingernail scratch somewhere other players won't notice it, which is usually anywhere.

What are the telltale signs of amateur card-markers? Start by looking for very long fingernails, and I'm not just talking about women. Some men you play poker with who have the unseemly habit of growing fingernails too long may not be as lazy as you think. Fingernails are an efficient and safe way to mark cards in home games. When the "marker" gets accused he can wiggle out of it by saying he unintentionally scratched the cards. Had he been caught with a hidden needle or some kind of "paint," then he would be as guilty as I am for telling you about it.

Other means of marking cards short of nomination to the cheaters hall of fame, of which I am, thank you, an inductee (didn't have to wait the five years either), include sharp edged or ridged jewelry, food crumbs that stain (lots of things normally served at the poker table can do this), food oils (potato-chip grease), and even poker chips! Yes, that's right. Since people are constantly fiddling with their chips, what better cover than to press one of them into the corner of an ace? That'll give the tip of the card a good crease.

Best way to spot card-markers? Be alert and keep everyone, including your proctologist who never misses a game, under a watchful eye. Also make sure that each deck of cards your game starts with is freshly sealed and not tampered with. Beware of crooked decks that have been pre-marked before packaged. Most of the patterns are easily discernible when looked for. The most common have clock patterns with a certain discoloration or tiny mark at each spot where the hour hand would be. These "clock decks" are easy to crack because the spots or dots are found at the corresponding time. For example, a mark at three o'clock means the card is a 3. Six o'clock would be a 6. Eleven o'clock indicates a jack, 11:30 a queen. High noon or midnight is a king, and one o'clock, you guessed it, the ace.

Another common pattern seen on the backs of marked cards is congruent designs that have a single discrepancy or disconnecting break at different spots along the length and width of the motif.

When passing in front of the naked eye, most of these unsophisticated marking patterns will escape detection, but on careful examination by that same naked eye, they normally jump up and volunteer their guilt.

Palming chips

Remember those magic tricks Sylvester was doing at your company's Christmas party? Well, watch out if Sylvester is part of your weekly poker game. He may be doing tricks without telling you, and they're costing you lots of money.

When does Sylvester do it? Most likely when he's making change from the pot or splitting the pot with another player at the end of a high–lowhigh–low hand.

How does Sylvester do it? It would be very easy for Sylvester to palm a chip or two, or three. No one would be the wiser, since chips, coins, and anything else that fits into the fleshy part of the human hand are very easily palmed by someone knowing how to do it.

How do you defend against chip-palmers? Well, just don't let them near the chips.

How do you do that?

Sorry, I don't know.

And by the way, the same talented people who palm chips might also be working the reverse of this scam by shorting pots. When calling a bet or a raise, they have the proper amount of chips in their hand, but when they throw them in the pot, one or two get stuck in their palm. This sneaky move can be prevented by forcing all players to cut out their chips in front of them before placing them in the pot, just like you see on TV tournaments.

Stalling and balking

There are always people who want to cheat in card games but don't have the skills necessary to do it. That is they don't have the physical agility to actively cheat. But they can sure pull the wool over your eyes by cheating passively.

How so? They will look for all sorts of angles to take advantage of you, so we'll call them "anglers" for the rest of this discussion. What they do is finagle with time, use its passage as a weapon against you. They are also masters of false body language...if having cards and chips used against you isn't bad enough!

Anglers know just when to delay or speed up their actions at the poker table in order to gain some information about you and your hand. Then by processing it, they alter or amend their own playing decisions. For example, a crude angling move would be when the angler gets you to throw away the winning hand without having to put up his chips.

In hold'em it works like this: the river card has just been placed on board and you have made a high pair. You think your hand might be good but you're not sure, so you don't bet. You figure, though, that the guy in position ahead of you will bet, as he had bet both the flop and the turn. You're willing to call him as the pot-odds justify tossing in one last bet. But then as all this is streaking through your mind, the player positioned behind you begins cutting out his chips as though preparing to raise, all the while giving off strong body language suggesting he's made the winning hand.

Now your strategy has been shaken. You think it over painfully. You still only have a high pair. Finally you say to yourself, "Ah, what the heck! I don't want to get involved with a raise which might be followed by a re-raise and even a re-re-raise." So you chuck your hand after the player in front of you bets. Lo and behold, the guy behind you who'd been playacting the raise just calls and beats out the player who'd bet. You feel pretty sick when you see that your hand, now lying in the muck, would have won the pot. The angler made a real schmuck out of you.

The savvy angler can also work the same scam from the other side. He might make you think that he's got nothing in an attempt to get you to raise the pot. He gives off all the negative signals of aggravation, tiredness, everything indicating a bad night at the table. Then you take the cue and bet the max, only to have him come over the top and get you to call another bet.

Best way to avoid being angled is to be on the lookout and maybe even do a little angling yourself. When an angler is confronted by someone else angling in the same game, he might just give up his act or go to another audition.

Misdeclaring hands

Another way a determined angler gains an advantage in home games is by misdeclaring his hand at showdown. Have you ever noticed that sometimes you think you have a spade flush but on closer examination you see that your fifth spade is actually a club? Or the last of five hearts turns like bad magic into a diamond. Well, misdeclaring artists notice this too, and they take advantage of it.

In friendly games people are always drinking, chatting and laughing, and no doubt most conversation has nothing to do with the poker game. The game itself is just a gathering place, no different than if you and your friends were partying it up while sliding a puck at bowling pins in a sawdust joint. This kindred atmosphere while playing poker lends excellent opportunities for deceptive players to take a shot at you, and if they're caught they can easily say they were just as drunk as you and misread their cards. And then everyone laughs it off, despite the fact that Peter tried to cheat Paul.

So next time you're in a big five-card draw or seven-card stud pot (this does not happen often in hold'em because each player is holding only two cards), and Billy on your right declares "flush," make sure you see his five suited cards before you throw your trips into the muck. In fact, the best way to stamp out cheap shots like this is to play "cards speak." Have each player involved in the pot turn his cards over in full view of everyone, just like they do in cardrooms.

Also beware of premeditated trickery when playing high–low split games. The sleight comes before showdown when each player must declare if he's going high or low. If your high–low split games are played "chip-declare," by which one chip in the fist means low and two high, watch out for the old two-loaded-fist trick, where the right fist has one chip and the left two, and the cheater waits a split second to see how you declared before showing you the fist he prefers: the right one when he has nothing but you went high; the left one when he has nothing and you went low.

That move, of course, is outright cheating. But then there are other types of devious maneuvering with declare-chips. A common one is a player jiggling two chips in his closed fist to make you believe he's about to declare high, but then at the last second he lets one of the chips slide out and goes low. A skilled chip-handler can also do this move after you've declared.

Remember Sylvester the magician from your Christmas party? If he's proved his skill of palming chips while making change from the pot, he'd surely be able to pull the old one-or-two-chips-in-the-fist trick.

Collusion teams working home games

Working collusion scams in home games is really venal and nasty but, nevertheless, it occurs. Let's say Ricky and Dicky are gambling buddies who often make the trek to the local casino or racetrack and fare about as well as little fish do in a tank filled with piranhas. So where do Ricky and Dicky get the money to keep themselves in action? Why not in their local Saturday night poker game? It's easy pickings taking the suckers to the cleaners.

Home-game collusion works more or less on the same principle as cardroom and online collusion, albeit the methods of passing information among the colluders are usually less sophisticated than those previously detailed for professional teams. If you come across any Rickys and Dickys in your own house game, the best way to nullify their collusion is to either form a counter-collusion team against them or post a sign on the basement door that says "NO COLLUDERS ALLOWED." They should get the message.

Of course, after reading about so many ways you can be cheated in your home game, you might be thinking that it's just a better idea to stay in your own home and get your poker thrills online, right? Well, I can't really say that. True, in today's online poker world you are relatively safe from all the non-colluding bandits out there. But should you ever run into a site on which crooked software is in use, then you would have been better off sitting in your home game with Tom, Louise, Billy, Sylvester and Ricky and Dicky, and letting them all cheat your pants off.

Chapter Eight

Great Poker Scams

The five greatest poker scams of all-time

The five and dime scam

A legendary gambler named Swifty Morgan roamed Manhattan's Lower East Side in the 1950s. Swifty was Irish but spent most of his time playing poker with his Italian and Jewish buddies who populated the neighborhood. Both the Italians and Jews knew Swifty was a degenerate gambler who oftentimes took up cheating to recover his losses. His specialty was marking cards, usually done in a crude way by filing down his overgrown thumbnail to a sharp edge. Several times Swifty was caught in the act, whereon the Italians and Jews alternated beating the shit out of him.

But they never barred him from the game because he was such a degenerate loser. The one rule they finally posted to prevent Swifty's cheating was to forbid him to bring cards to the games. All decks would be furnished by whichever Italian or Jew hosted the game.

Swifty had a hotblooded Irish temper, and he got pissed off real quickly when he started losing. During a two-month span in the 1955, Swifty's losing streak took on wacky proportions. He'd finally had enough of losing his bankroll to the Italians and Jews, so he came up with a plan not only to get even with them but to take their bankrolls as well.

There was a small five and dime store in the neighborhood that stayed open until midnight. It was about the only place of commerce that wasn't closed by nine o'clock. The last time Swifty had been there, he noticed that playing cards were on sale.

One wintry afternoon, Swifty walked inside the store at five o'clock. He went directly to the shelf where the cards were displayed and bought half the supply of Bicycle decks. He took the cards home, and using a knife with a very thin blade removed the cellophane wrapping on the boxes, paying special attention to leave the store's price tags in place and undamaged. He then carefully slid the wrapping off the first box, leaving the cellophane intact. He used a razor blade to cut open the side of the box, leaving the blue sealing stamp in place on the box's flap. He removed the cards and began skillfully marking their backs with tiny applications of a daub he'd bought in a novelty store.

Finished marking, he placed the cards back in the box, reglued the open side and very carefully slid the cellophane wrapper over the freshly resealed box. After refolding the wrapper to the exact way it appeared before he'd slit it, Swifty fetched a cloth and laid it over the cellophane. Then he pressed a hot iron lightly against the cloth, sealing the cellophane. On final examination of his work, Swifty was satisfied that the deck, still sealed in cellophane and protected by the blue stamp, appeared as though he'd never opened it.

Swifty repeated this process for another 19 decks. Then he immediately returned to the five and dime store. When the owner wasn't looking, he scooped the remaining decks on the shelf and dropped them into his sack. Then he restocked the shelf with the 20 decks he'd marked at home. Now every deck of playing cards for sale at the five and dime was marked.

That night, Swifty went to one of the Jew's houses in the neighborhood. He was swiftly searched by both the Jew and one of the Italians before they allowed him inside. He had no marked cards or cheating paraphernalia of any kind on his person. He was led to the eight-handed poker game upstairs.

The game of choice was five-card stud. The stakes were $10–20, a pretty steep game for the times. It started at nine o'clock. After half an hour of play, Swifty was stuck $200. By ten he was stuck $350. Growing angrier by the minute and adding a bit of theatrics to his outburst, Swifty had enough. After a losing hand, he tore up his cards.

"Whaddidya do that for, you little twerp!" cried one of the Italians.

"Never mind," Swifty said indignantly. "I won't do it again."

The host of the game fetched a new deck of cards and dealt out the next hand. Swifty lost on purpose. When one of the Jews threw over his winning hole card, Swifty ripped up his cards again.

"Whaddidya do that for, you little asshole!" cried the Jew who won the pot.

"Never mind," Swifty said indignantly. "I won't do it again. This time I promise."

"You won't do it again?" cried the host. "You *can't* do it again. I don't have any more decks of cards!"

"You don't have any more decks?" another of the Italians asked in a voice filled with panic. "How we gonna continue?"

"Looks like we're fucked," the host observed. Pointing at Swifty he added, "Because of this little Irish piss-ass."

"Does anyone have any cards on them?" someone asked.

"I would've brought some," Swifty replied quickly. "But

you guys forbade me to bring cards."

"Shut up, asshole!" the meanest of the Italians said. Then to everyone: "None of yuz got any cards?"

Everyone shook his head.

"Shit!" hollered the last Jew. "We can't even buy any cards. There ain't nothin' in this shithole neighborhood open past nine o'clock."

At this point Swifty looked around the room longingly, preying he'd hear the magic words.

"Wait a minute!" the host said in a burst of sudden excitement. "The five and dime on Fourteenth Street! I forget the name of it, but I think it's open until midnight...Yeah, it is! I bought some lozenges there one night when my mother had a sore throat. They sell cards!"

An instant later, the last Italian, who was also the fastest runner of the bunch, was out the door on his way to the five and dime. He was back five minutes later with two decks of pretty blue-backed Bicycle playing cards.

Three hours later, Swifty had all their money.

The Italians and the Jews beat the hell out of him on his way out the door. But not because they discovered the marked cards. They just got pissed off that Swifty was leaving with their money.

The printing press scam

You're probably thinking that this one has something to do with counterfeiting money. Well, no, it's not even about counterfeiting cards, but it is about marking them.

The Baden-Baden casino in Germany is perhaps the most beautiful gambling palace in the entire world. When I was there with my pastposting team in 1997, I was so awed by the place that I couldn't bring myself to do a move on its tables. The casino was more than just a casino; it was an art museum.

Inside, below lustrous chandeliers hanging from towering ceilings were separate regal gaming rooms whose walls were lined with works of art by the masters. One of these rooms was reserved for a high-stakes poker game attended by European nobility from all over the continent.

The Baden-Baden poker game basked in the glory of its heyday in the 1870s when the famed Russian writer Dostoyevsky whiled away more time in the casino's crowded roulette room than he did penning manuscripts. When his numbers went cold, Dostoyevsky was known to stroll up to the poker game and take a seat.

The casino supplied majestic European-style playing cards that were produced by a printer who was actually a descendant of Gutenberg and whose printing shop was located just five miles by carriage from the regal casino.

Well, as the story goes, one of the princes playing in this game was a degenerate gambler who lost so much money that he endangered both his castle and his princess. He was running up astonishing debts to the rest of the nobility in the game, which threatened to create a big enough scandal to aggravate even King Ludwig, who was already considered apathetically insane by many Bavarians. The prince didn't know what to do, but one night while alone in his castle (his princess, furious with him for his gambling losses, had run off with a caretaker) he had a brainstorm.

On a brisk, sunny fall afternoon, after another losing session at the poker game, the prince instructed his carriage chauffeur to take him to see the printer. After formalities were exchanged, he advised the printer that he had written a special poem of apology for the princess and wanted the printer to reproduce it with his most elegant calligraphy. But it was all a load of crap. What the prince wanted was a tour of the printer's facilities, which he got from a very obliging printer who knew he would charge the prince a pretty shilling or two for his work.

Later that night, the prince drove his own carriage to the print shop, sneaked inside it and secretly altered the engraving plates the printer used to produce the playing cards for the Baden-Baden casino. The plan was that the printer would unknowingly supply Baden-Baden with marked cards.

At the time, cards were not nearly as mass produced as they are today, so the prince would have to wait a few weeks before the marked decks hit the poker table. He resisted all temptation and managed to stay away from the casino until he knew the marked cards were in play. In the interim he even had the good fortune to win back the princess, who found out that the caretaker had been two-timing *her*.

Naturally the prince went on a fabulous winning streak at the Baden-Baden high-stakes poker table. He busted out a collection of counts, viceroys, dukes, earls and even the great Dostoyevsky. In fact, he put such a hurt on Dostoyevsky that the famed Russian writer was forced to go home to Russia and write *The Gambler*, for which he received enough money to return to Baden-Baden and seek his revenge against the prince.

When Dostoyevsky returned to the casino, the marked cards were still in play. It didn't take long for the prince to send him packing again. After writing yet another book to finance still another gambling binge, Dostoyevsky returned to the poker table yet again. This time, after losing the great Russian writer jumped up and accused the prince of cheating. When the prince, filled with indignation, demanded of Dostoyevsky to produce evidence backing up his accusation, the writer laid the printer's business card on the table.

Stunned, the prince asked, "How did you know?"

Dostoyevsky replied, "I did the same thing but the idiot sent my cards to the wrong casino."

The double-rake scam

In the 1890s, San Francisco's Barbary Coast overflowed with gambling action. Many people don't know this but the City on the Bay was actually a precursor of Las Vegas. The first casino slot machines were invented and put to use along its waterfront gambling halls.

Like in all American gambling venues, poker found its home on the Barbary Coast. Ever since the Gold Rush, players flocked in droves to try their luck and skill on the new frontier's poker tables. Gamblers came from New Orleans, Steubenville, and even Alaska to get in on the action. Many enjoyed the Coast's row of watering holes as well.

One person who recognized that most of the poker players became drunk by the morning wee hours was an enterprizing lady dealer named Babs. Her shift began in the early evening and didn't end until enough players went broke to stall the game. Babs dealt five-card stud, just as she had in New Orleans before coming out west.

Her husband was an experienced laborer who had a special talent for constructing gizmos that worked on pulleys, springs and levers. Like his wife, he also had a penchant for high living, but also like his wife he was always short of cash. Together they hatched a plot.

Babs' game worked on a rake from each contested pot. She was responsible to remove the chips due the house before pushing the pot to the winning player. The rake varied from 1% to 3% depending on the particular game and how drunk her players were. It was in carrying out this function that Babs realized she could further rake the pot for her own benefit. If hubby could produce the tool, she'd produce the cash.

The tool was a hollow white cylinder that looked like a small stack of white $1 chips. It had a bottom base that moved inward on springs. By lightly pressing the top end of the cylinder to activate the springs on the bottom, Babs was able to suck up three $1 chips in the dark while supposedly removing only the $1 chips needed to satisfy the game's rake.

She did this every hand, unless someone was causing her to feel heat. Her game was loaded with action that made big pots, so no one noticed the three $1 chips she siphoned off every pot. At 20 pots an hour, Babs had taken down $60 each time her watch's minute hand struck 12. That amounted to $500 a shift, four grand a week when she worked seven days, a real fortune in 1890s America.

Babs continued her double-rake scam unimpeded. She and hubby began living in secret luxury, richly decorating the inside of what from the outside appeared to be their modest home. Together they dined in fine restaurants, frequented the opera, attended ballet performances, enjoyed piano recitals in private hotel suites and sat in the orchestra while viewing stage plays. Alone, each indulged in private fantasies with or without the spouse's knowledge. At the poker table no one seemed to have a clue. Babs and hubby began to believe it could go on forever.

Forever ended abruptly one night when Babs pressed the top end of the cylinder to suck in the chips and was shocked to see her index finger go right through the top into the cylinder. The top had collapsed. Babs' first thought was that it wasn't so bad. Hubby could either repair the device or build a new one. But what Babs hadn't noticed those first few moments was that her finger had been gripped by the snaking coils inside the cylinder and could not be dislodged. True to her coolness under pressure, Babs did not panic. She tried to continue dealing the game with the cylinder sticking onto her fingertip like a white thimble. She gamely carried on for a few hands but finally one of the drunken players asked her if she'd been sewing during her break.

Shortly afterward, Babs and her husband disappeared from the Barbary Coast. Rumor had it that they had been packed into a large cylinder, similar in shape to the one Babs had used on the poker game, that is still weighted down somewhere on the bottom of the San Francisco Bay.

The O'Leary scam

My favorite scam was not exactly a poker scam, but it was so good I must include it on the list. Probably because *I* was the victim.

One night 20 years ago while getting drunk in a New York Irish pub, the conversation turned to gambling and card playing. I was there with a girl I'd met hours before in another pub that might also have been an Irish one; I can't remember. There were 20 or so people engaged in this conversation and it was quite lively. Two Irish guys—I mean real Irish guys from Ireland with red hair, white skin and freckles— had everyone cracking up with their little gambling anecdotes leading to one catastrophe or another. Then a woman who was plainly Italian pulled a deck of cards and slapped them on the bar.

"Anyone want to see a great card trick?" she beamed, probably at least as sauced as I was.

Everyone pitched in with encouraging laughter to say how thrilled everyone else would be to see her card trick. She then proceeded to do that classic dopey poker-hand trick everyone has seen performed by at least four generations of his family: the one with the four hands of seven-stud ending up four jacks, four queens, four kings and, of course, four aces for the dealer.

Everybody applauded her, anyway, and then another schmuck took the cards and began shuffling. When he'd finished, he dealt three columns of seven cards face up. He said to the girl who'd just finished her crummy trick, "Pick a card, but don't tell me what it is. Keep it in your head."

The girl was either stupid enough or drunk enough to blurt, "Does it have to be one of the cards you dealt on the bar?" The rest of the deck was lying off to the side.

The guy indulged her with a smiling nod. She was kind of hot and had big tits, so obviously he didn't care how dumb she was.

The girl's drunken eyes passed over the 21 cards. "Okay, I chose a card."

I recognized the trick as soon as the guy started dealing out the columns. It was one of those mathematical numbers that could never go wrong if you didn't fuck up the procedure. The version he was doing was the one with the petals and the flowers, goading the victim to pick this petal then that one after she'd already picked the two columns that didn't contain the card. I think the first time I saw the trick done was in kindergarten.

The woman, ever so drunk as she was, managed to play along and finished by affirming that the card the guy flicked over at the end was indeed hers.

I'd just about had my share of card tricks when one of the two redheaded Irish guys clamored, "Those tricks are for bloody boobheads!" Anyone here want to see a real good one?"

For some reason I volunteered, surely hoping it would be better than the previous two and the last of the night.

He picked up the deck off the bar and fanned them face up in front of me. "Pick any card," he said.

I looked at him. "Just like that, face up?"

The other Irish guy piped in behind him. "Yeah, mate, just like that."

I slid out the 9♠ without hesitation. I looked up waiting for one of them to do something.

The one next to me spoke. "What would you say if I told you I know someone back in Ireland whom I could call right now, hand him the phone without saying a word, and he'll tell you that the card you picked was the 9 of spades?"

I looked at my watch. It was eleven o'clock at night in New York, which meant it was four o'clock the next morning in Ireland.

"I'd say the guy either goes to bed late or gets up early."

They laughed heartily, then the one behind suggested slyly, "Care to make a little wager on that, mate?"

I looked at the girl I was with. I could see she knew as much about cards as I did about the theory of relativity, which was zero.

"Come on, mate," the one who'd spread the cards said. "Why not put a little fun in the evening. Soon it'll be the top of the mornin'."

"Okay," I said pulling out my wallet. "I'll go 20 bucks saying your friend in Ireland can't tell me my card if you don't tip him off."

"Twenty bucks!" they exclaimed in unison. Then they took turns telling me I insulted their chivalrous play. The one behind finished off with, "The phone call over there will hardly be covered for 20 bucks, mate."

Well, whatever their gig was, it was clear they knew I'd lose the bet. And this in spite of the fact they didn't know whom they were trying to hustle. But I was curious about their trick, plus I was in a good mood knowing I was going to get laid once I got out of there.

"So how much do I have to do this for?" I asked them.

"You got 50?"

"Sure." I laid the 50 on the bar. They did not hesitate to lay theirs alongside it. "Now let's make that call."

You have to remember that 20 years ago there were no cell

phones. There was just a cranky old pay phone near the entrance. The front guy asked the bartender, "Pat, gimme 10 bucks in quarters, would ya?"

"It's okay," Pat chimed, you can use the bar phone." He reached underneath the bar, pulled it out and slapped it on the surface next to the nine of spades. "Who you calling, anyway?"

"Some bloke in Ireland."

The phone slid off the bar and disappeared faster than you could say "Dublin."

I followed the two Irishmen to the pay phone. At least 10 people followed me, everyone with either a drink or cigarette in his hand. As the one dropped a load of quarters into the phone's slot, he piped at me, "Are you ready, mate?"

I nodded.

"I'm not going to say a word to my buddy on the phone about your card. I'll just see if he's home and pass you the phone when he comes on. Okay?"

"Okay."

He dialed a number, then after a few seconds said into the receiver, "Is Mr. O'Leary there?" Then he said, "Hold on," and passed me the phone.

I put the receiver to my ear. "Mr. O'Leary?"

The cheery voice on the other end was indeed Irish. "That's me, mate. Your card is the 9 of spades."

At first I thought it no big deal that he knew my card, but when it finally hit me that he *knew* my card I was flabbergasted. For some reason I thanked him before hanging up.

When I turned back to the two Irishman, they were already at the bar scooping up my $50 bill. Everyone else was asking if the guy on the phone guessed my card.

"He didn't guess it," I informed the crowd with a bit of thespian delight. "He knew it."

The two Irish guys were laughing as I came over. "You want to do it again, mate?" one of them asked.

"Yeah," I answered immediately, "but how 'bout for less money." I knew that I was outhustled but I wanted to see this again, figure out how they did it. I knew they wouldn't give it up for nothing.

"Okay," the second one said as he picked up the cards and gave them a quick shuffle with a fancy bridge. He spread them and told me to pick a card. I fingered the width of the fanned cards and slipped out the 4♣. Then the first Irishman put a 20-dollar bill on the bar and told me to match it.

I laid the bill on the bar and followed them back to the phone. Evidently enough quarters remained in the Irishman's pocket to make the second call. He dialed and again asked for Mr. O'Leary. When O'Leary came on the line, he told him to hold on and passed me the receiver. I bade the familiar voice hello and he answered with "Your card is the four of clubs."

"Wanna go again, mate?" The Irish guys were having a ball with me.

"How the fuck did you guys do that?" I demanded.

The first one gave me a peppered shrug and said, "You know magicians don't give away their secrets."

"It's not magic," I protested. "It's a goddamn card trick."

The second one had a great retort for that. "It's not a trick. O'Leary just read your mind. He knows you're thinking of your card when you get on the phone. So he just hones in on your brain and finds the part of it thinking of the card."

"You guys got a good line of shit," I said, and they got off laughing at me. The whole bar was getting in on it, including the bartender who seemed to have already borne witness to their little gag. I approached the bartender and asked him how they did it. He just chuckled and said in an Irish accent, "I haven't the foggiest idea, mate?"

How the hell *did* they do it? That thought prevented me from both getting laid and sleeping that night. I lay awake for hours in the girl's apartment, in her bed with her lovely body sprawled naked in the same spot where she'd finally given up on me and fallen asleep.

Not only am I a fairly intelligent person but I know how to navigate pretty well around logic. The first thing I was sure of was that somehow that Irish guy in the bar told Mr. O'Leary what my card was. The only way that certainty would not be true was if there had been another unseen phone extension inside the bar and somebody else told Mr. O'Leary the card. But after being led on a tour of the place by the bartender, during which I felt like an idiot, I had to accept the fact there was no other phone on the property.

So then how did the Irish guy tell O'Leary which card I'd selected? I had been right by his side when they spoke. Twice. Each time, the Irish guy said nothing more than "Is Mr. O'Leary there?" and "hold on." Neither utterance contained words that would indicate the 9 of spades and the 4 of clubs. But somehow those words did indicate those cards. And it was killing me to find out.

I racked my brains. Somewhere in those lines was a hidden code that told Mr. O'Leary what my cards were. But how could the same exact lines give him the correct information for two different cards? I even asked myself if it were possible that the inflection in the caller's voice tipped off O'Leary. But if that were the case then O'Leary would have to be sensitive to 52 different inflections. Impossible.

The unknown solution ate at me an entire week. Then finally, not being able to take it any more, I returned to the pub on a busy Saturday night. The place was packed, and sure enough the two Irish guys were hustling another customer with their trick. Only this time the bills on the bar were hundreds and the guy getting taken was sweating and did not look happy.

I watched all this from a distance. The Irish guys either didn't see me or didn't recognize me. The victim followed them to the phone, probably for the second or third time, and on hanging up came walking back toward the bar in disbelief, then did an about-face toward the exit. The second he was out the door, I saw one of the Irish guys pass a bill off to the bartender, who promptly stuck it in his pocket.

So the bartender was in on it as well. They were working a major scam with this trick, or whatever the hell it was.

I came back the next night determined to crack the case. Irish pubs in Manhattan usually drew crowds every night of the week. Sunday night at this one was no exception. The Irish guys were flirting with a couple of women by the bar. I decided to wait patiently until they went into the routine. I knew they would eventually because these guys were not there for just booze and broads. The place was their livelihood.

At midnight, just before I was about to pack it in, two slick looking black dudes walked inside the bar. They had that instant air of loose cash, either pro athletes or musicians. The Irish pair adroitly got them into conversation and within a half hour the bar top was crawling with $100 bills. I was thinking to myself that the scammers had better be careful with these black guys. They looked like the kind you didn't want to mess with. But obviously the Irish duo was very well rounded and knew how to handle whatever situation arose during the working of the scam.

Well, we'll see about that, I said to myself.

As soon as the Irish guy dropped the quarters into the phone's slot, I made my way through the thinning crowd toward him. I watched him dial and waited until I knew instinctively that the moment had arrived to make my move. I charged the pay phone and grabbed the receiver from the guy's hand. He protested but I quickly knocked him out of the way. I then put the receiver to my ear without uttering a sound. What I heard at first made no sense. It was indeed O'Leary's voice and it was counting..."two, three four, five, six..."

The Irish guy made a lunge at me but I knocked him out of the way again. His buddy was coming after me too, but one of the black dudes stuck out a big arm and held him at bay. By that time O'Leary had reached "king." And then his voice rasped in my ear, "What's the fucking card, mate! Did I miss it?"

"You sure did, scumbag!" and I hung up the phone.

There's an old New York joke about asking a bartender what time his Irish pub closes. He doesn't answer you with a time; rather he says, "As soon as the first fistfight breaks out."

Well, that meant this Irish pub would be closing real soon. In the ensuing brawl I got whacked with a few good shots that drew blood from my mouth. The poor Irish guys, whose names turned out to be Ian and Donald Lorrigan and who were currently on their way to the hospital ward at the Riker's Island jail, got the shit kicked out of them. I was also in lots of pain, but at least it had not been for nothing. I paid the price but I figured out their scam.

The arresting cops asked me what it was all about, and when I told them, one of the coppers, who was also Irish, quipped, "Musta been a pretty good card trick."

It was simply the best card trick I had ever seen. The way it worked was in reversal. It was true that the caller was transmitting the information to O'Leary, but he was doing it in reverse. That's why virtually no one can figure it out.

The key to deciphering it is that you have to know it was

O'Leary speaking first, not the Irish guy. The first words I had heard from the caller were "Is Mr. O'Leary there?" On hearing those words you naturally assume that whoever answered on the other end had picked up with a "hello" or something to that effect. Then when the Irish guy says "Hold on" and passes the phone off to the victim, you naturally think that O'Leary had just come to the phone after having been summoned by the person who had picked it up.

But it is really O'Leary who answers the phone. Instead of saying hello, he goes right into a recital of counting the cards..."ace, 2, 3, 4..." Then when he arrives at the card you had chosen, the caller says "Is Mr. O'Leary there?" That stops O'Leary's counting dead in its tracks. For if the last card O'Leary said was "jack," then he knows it's a jack.

Next only the correct suit needs to be transmitted. Once O'Leary receives the signal that the card is a jack, he begins reciting the four suits..."spades, clubs, hearts, diamonds." As soon as he hits the correct one, the caller says "Hold on," which tells O'Leary he just said the right suit, and passes the phone to the victim who's about to be stunned.

What makes this trick so unbelievable is how natural the talking sounds. The set-up guy just dials a number, asks to speak with someone and then asks that person to hold on while he passes the phone to the victim. I had never been so impressed by a card trick or phone trick, whatever you want to call it. Learning it was well worth the 70 bucks I lost and the busted lip.

Over the years I've done that trick dozens of times, though never for profit. The most fun performing it is at parties or anyplace with large gatherings of people. Listening to people trying to figure it out is as funny as any comedy routine you'll ever see. The ridiculous theories people put forth to solve the puzzle are as unreal as they are hilarious. You hear everything from high-tech satellites eavesdropping on the room to infrared lenses spying on the deck of cards from another galaxy.

One time at a party while doing the trick, a cute girl made me come with her into the bathroom with the lights off. She said she wanted to be sure that no one else could see which card she chose. I wondered if it was a pretext to jump my bones, but when she struck a match to create a small light while she picked the card, I realized how nuts this trick drove everybody, as it had once done to me.

The novice scam

One of the greatest gambling scams of all-time did not take place at a poker table but it was certainly hatched on one. Believe it or not, it happened onboard the *Titanic*, two days before the great ship hit the iceberg. The guy who pulled it off went down with the vessel, but before dying he recounted the scam to a young stowaway as they lay clinging to a life raft in the icy waters of the North Atlantic. The first thing the bowled over lad did on his rescue was to tell anyone else who'd listen.

Among Europe's elite and wealthy on the passenger manifest for that fateful voyage was a good old Anglo-Saxon con artist. His name was Piers Mason and he was as dashing and charming as they came. He travelled with a well-heeled and very attractive woman named Isabel, who for some reason resented the upper crust of society and liked teaming up with Mason to rip off its elegant members.

Mason was quite aware of the roster of fortune holders making that historical crossing and wasn't going to miss it for the world. He had called in all his markers and then begged, borrowed and stole every penny of front money he could, without knowing exactly how he'd use it on the ship. The one part of his plan he was sure of was that removing those rich pigeons from their money had to be done through some form of gambling.

Like the riverboats steaming down the Mississippi, the principal form of gambling on the gigantic ocean liner was poker. The nightly high-stakes game onboard was filled with barons, earls and varied aristocrats who fawned on each other in several languages, most of which Mason spoke fluently. His first idea was to slip a marked deck of cards into play and thieve his noble opponents by reading their hole cards. But some of these people were sharp (after all, those who make fortunes are usually not idiots) and might notice the markings. In those days, specially made eyeglasses or contact lenses for card scams did not exist.

Isabel and Mason had been in their stateroom dressing into formal evening attire when Piers suddenly called off his plan to mark the cards.

"But how else are you going to get their money, honey?" Isabel asked with comic but great concern.

"I don't know but I'll figure it out while I'm playing."

"Playing?"

"That's right." Mason's confidence, like that of all con men, was unshakeable.

"But darling," Isabel said with a seductive rub embracing his shoulders. "How can you play honestly with them? Our bankroll is only £50,000."

"I will play conservatively," Mason assured her. "It's only my presence in the game that is important. While sitting there among all that blue blood I will figure something out. Trust me."

She did and he did...figure something out.

Stuck nearly £10,000 that first night at the gilded poker table, Mason picked up an interesting tidbit in the lofty chatter flowing across the table. Aboard the ship were two chess grandmasters on their way to a prestigious chess tournament in New York. One was Russian, the other German. Both had been invited to take part in the poker game but both professed to be too busy studying their chess strategies and declined.

At a well-chosen moment in the game, Mason, who had by that time ingratiated himself into their crisscrossing conversations, made a statement that none of the regal gentlemen could believe.

"My fiancée can play and hold her own with either grandmaster," he declared like a bellicose general who knew his troops would recapture the hill.

None of the poker players at first believed his ears, but finally one of them asked Piers to clarify what he meant. When Mason repeated it, another of the players said in amazement, "You think your...fiancée can play chess with Borzov and Heilmann?" Borzov was the Russian, Heilmann the German.

"I'm sure of it," Mason said in a steely voice, all the while knowing that Isabel had never touched a chess piece in her life.

After a hearty round of chuckling, one of the nobility said to Mason, "Would you care to wager on that? I'm sure I can convince Messieurs Borzov and Heilmann to accept an invitation for a match."

"I will tell you what," Mason said boldly. "I will have my fiancée play both grandmasters. I will stake £40,000 (all he had left) that she attains a stalemate with at least one of them."

They all laughed again. Uproariously. Finally one asked, "Well, then, which of the two grandmasters would your fiancee play first?" He looked around the table seeking mock assurance it was a good question.

Mason shrugged grandly. "She will play both simultane-ously."

Again the laughter roared.

"Simultaneously?" It was a chorus.

"Yes, simultaneously," Piers repeated for effect.

The majestic group thought the emboldened con man was off his rocker, but the last thing they thought was that he was a con man. After a few more rounds of belly laughter, a wealthy retired British admiral hushed his high-society fellows and stood up at the table facing Mason. He gave the con artist a lookover and then smiled.

"You're quite a dapper young man," he said to him, "but I think you've lost your marbles. Do you really want to wager £40,000 that your girlfr...fiancée can earn a stalemate against either Borzov or Heilmann, two of the greatest grandmasters in the world?"

Mason stood up and met the admiral's gaze. "Yes, I do."

The admiral's eyes scanned the men seated below him at the table. Then to Piers, "Mind if I inquire how much money you've brought along on this journey?"

"My life savings," Mason answered proudly.

After a collective exhalation of shock, the admiral asked, "And how much would that be?"

"£50,000." But Mason did not let it be known that the totality of that sum had been made up of loans and stolen booty.

"And you want to wager £40,000 of it?"

"I've already lost the other 10." Mason indicated the poker table, which drew a guffaw from the men seated around it.

The admiral smiled broadly. "If there's one thing I admire within His Majesty's realm it's one of his subjects with big brass balls. And those, young man, you seem to have. So I'll tell you what I'm going to do. I'm going to arrange simultaneous matches between your fiancee...what's her name?"

"Isabel."

"...Isabel...and both chess masters. If Isabel achieves a stalemate with either one, I will give you £100,000. You don't need to put up one penny. If she *wins* one of the matches, I will pay you £1 million. I won't bother mentioning the possibility of her winning both matches because I can't even believe I had the audacity to suggest that her winning one is somehow possible."

Piers nodded politely. "And if she loses both matches I owe you nothing?"

The admiral looked around the table as if for concurrence. He seemed to get it. He nodded graciously. "Yes, though I would expect you'd buy us all a glass of champagne and cognac."

So the admiral and his regal mates set out to organize the match. Naturally Borzov and Heilmann, who each had the large ego typical of any chess grandmaster, were loath to lower themselves to a match with "some unknown woman." But the admiral promised to sweeten their pies should they indulge him. It seemed he was a man who knew no limit when it came to entertaining himself.

At dinner the evening of the match, the atmosphere buzzed with anticipation of the event. Nobody took the match itself seriously, with the exception of Mason, but nearly everyone was just dying of curiosity to see who this mysterious if not talented woman could be. Mason had already paid off stewards working the cruise to spread the word that she was extremely beautiful, which was only a slight exaggeration.

The tables were set up in the ship's grand ballroom. A partition separated them. It was agreed that one-minute intervals would be the maximum between moves. The only request Mason had made of the admiral was that spectators be prohibited from viewing both matches. He explained that Isabel's concentration would be thrown if people were watching and commenting on her play in two different matches. The admiral, after discussing the request briefly with his peers, consented. The grandmasters as well saw no reason for objection, though they expressed their consent with derisive chuckles.

So chairs for the spectators were set up in such a way that allowed them to view only one of the two matches.

When Isabel made her grand entrance wearing a beautifully tailored, exquisite white evening gown, the audience buzzed first with sighs of delightful approval and then in hushed banter about whether or not this striking woman could play chess. At the time, women had not made noteworthy inroads or contributions to the chess world, and according to Borzov and Heilmann never would.

The match with Borzov started first. The Russian played white, so in all fairness Isabel would play white against Heilmann. Borzov opened by advancing a white pawn. Isabel studied the board with a seemingly practiced eye, then suddenly stood up without touching a piece and gracefully skirted the partition to stand across the board from the German. She made her opening move, waited for Heilmann's countermove and then returned to her match with Borzov.

Isabel did not sit down again. She moved with poise from table to table, never coming close to the one-minute limit on the clock. After 10 minutes, it appeared to everyone on both sides of the partition that Isabel was holding her own and would be no pushover for either opponent. The spectators appeared astounded. The only person not looking amazed by the events unfolding was Piers Mason, and he was also the only spectator aboard the *Titanic* who knew that before this grand evening of chess, his graceful protégée had never seen a chessboard that was not on display in some fancy store's vitrine.

Thirty minutes into the matches, Heilmann began to show visible signs of distress. Beads of perspiration began seeping out on his forehead. Not being able to put away an unknown chess opponent was bad enough, but not being able to win out over a woman was a sheer blow to his Teutonic pride. He would not be able to face his friends in the beer halls of Munich. How on heaven's earth was this woman staying in the match with him?

The admiral, although he seemed amused by the idea of shelling out a barrel of cash should this woman reach a stalemate or better with one of her opponents, seemed to be in the grips of stupefaction.

After an hour, the Russian began coming apart as well. He knew he was playing white, which afforded him the advantage against any player in the world, even those who might be slightly better than him. But in spite of that, each and every offensive move he made was countered perfectly by this beautiful woman. How was this possible? How could he show his face to the genteel New Yorkers at the chess tournament? If news got out he couldn't beat some woman on a boat, no matter how goddamn big the *Titanic* was, he might as well just walk outside to the deck, peer into the darkness of the ocean and....

Soon Heilmann was beside himself. He'd played against the world's best. He'd seen every schematic opening, knew the histories and subtleties of each. They were all vulnerable once the slightest miscalculation was made by the player with white. Virtually every opponent he'd played black against made the slight error Heilmann needed to turn his defending black chessmen into an offensive onslaught.

But not against this woman! Not...what was her name again? Her offensive attack was relentless. All he could do was ward off her thrusts and hang on. And that was only to attain the stalemate. He was leaps and bounds away from thinking about winning. *Leaps and bounds!* This was madness!

Nearing the end, both grandmasters knew they were help-lessly deadlocked with their opponent. It was unthinkable but it was happening. However, the Russian playing white still knew he couldn't lose the match, therefore would never ac-cept a stalemate. The German, on the other hand, was begin-ning to believe he could never win the match, and if he lost it (unaware that an iceberg would soon end his embarrassment) would actually contemplate suicide.

In the most humbling moment of his life, the grandmaster Heilmann offered his lovely opponent a draw.

None of the three chess players survived the catastrophic accident to live in the aftermath of that unforgettable night of chess. Neither did Piers Mason. He froze to death clinging onto the raft in icy waters. Only the stowaway Mason con-fided in before dying would live to tell how Piers and Isabel did it. Mason had told the kid only because he wanted him to brag about it so that everyone in England would remember Piers Mason for having pulled off the greatest scam in mari-time history.

I think he did.

Like any fantastic hustle, its beauty was in its simplicity. The fact that Isabel didn't even know how to move the knight had no bearing on the outcome. Mason's brainstorm was in recognizing that by having the two matches partitioned off from each other, he could effectively pit Borzov against Heil-mann, with Isabel's role in the challenge being nothing more than a mere messenger between the two. And they managed to keep the audience in the dark as to what was going down.

The key to making the scam work was threefold: having Isabel play white against one opponent and black against the other; having the opponent playing black make his first move before Isabel made her first move with black against the opponent playing white; and allowing a sufficient interval between moves. In that fashion, Isabel was able to get up and prance between the two tables for a full minute before having to make a move.

But she hardly needed the full minute. All Isabel did was take each move Borzov made against her and copy it to the adjoining chessboard against Heilmann. Then when Heilmann countered, she simply took his move and copied it to the chessboard between her and Borzov. The result of this chicanery was that Borzov and Heilmann were engaged in a chess match against each other and neither knew it. To further enhance the scam, Mason came up with the idea to disallow the viewing of both matches by anyone, thus no one could spill the beans that Isabel was plagiarizing both players' moves.

The scam was truly ingenious. In my 25 years of developing fundamentally sound cheating moves, I strove to come up with those that were simple because simplicity always works best. It may seem astonishing that two great minds such as Borzov's and Heilmann's were unable to fathom how Isabel had managed the stalemates, even more so when the odds of that miracle were in the neighborhood of infinity. But as the grandmasters were so obsessed by their chess-playing and their egos, the idea that the matches might have been a scam never occurred to either genius. I'm sure if they've read this passage, they've rolled over in their graves.

The best poker scam never done

This is one that would net its perpetrators a cool $7,500,000. At least that's what the take would have been had the scam taken place on July 16, 2005. Does that amount ring a bell? How about the date? Can you figure it out?

Okay, congratulations, you've come to the conclusion that this yet undone fantastic scam has something to do with the championship event at the World Series of Poker. So you ask if winning it is a scam? Well, yes and no. I've already told you what I know about that, but what I have in mind has nothing to do with playing poker.

It's a heist! Of course it's a heist. That's the best way to get the seven and a half mil without having to look at a goddamn poker hand, ain't it? After all, how many movies have we already seen depicting casino heists? Let's see: there are the two "Ocean's" movies with George Clooney and Brad Pitt, though the sequel doesn't have much to do with heisting casinos, even if it did evolve from the original remake. Then there's Nick Nolte in *The Good Thief* and of course the French classic *Mélodie en sous-sol* with Jean Gabin and Alain Delon, my favorite film. I used to rent it after a hard night's work kicking some French Riviera casino ass, and then go back to the hotel room and chill out while watching it.

But these are just movies. True, there have been some dazzling real-life casino heists, like the 1980s Vegas job engineered by a Stardust security guard who set up his own casino cage to be hit, but then got caught when the FBI found Stardust money wrappers from the booty in his kitchen cookie jar. In the 90s, LA drug gangs bombarded the Las Vegas strip with brazen casino robberies at about the same time Heather Tallchief, an employee for an armored car company who's in the process of selling her story to Hollywood, drove off with three million bucks while her partners were left standing outside the casino holding empty bags. However, none of these ballsy jobs netted anywhere near the $7.5 million I'm talking about now.

You've finally figured it out! Yes, that's right. I'm talking about heisting the final table at the World Series of Poker, right at the end when the tournament officials pile up those bricks of $7.5 million in cash on the table! You think I'm crazy? Why not heist the World Series? The haul would certainly be the biggest in Las Vegas history, at least at the time of the crime. Shit, it would be in the same class as the infamous Lufthansa heist at JFK Airport, and they'd probably make a movie about it starring De Niro. All you and your *colluders* for this one would need is a few sets—not of aces, but of balls.

Now you ask me how to do it? Hey, wait a minute! You know I've always been a classy thief. I've always managed to remove casinos from their money with a touch of class. But a heist? Or maybe it's not a heist after all. Maybe you guys can figure out a way to pull it off through massive deception and artful distraction. I don't know, but all I can tell you is that if you get away with it, you've not only earned my respect but you've played one hell of a hand.

Now that, my friends, is dirty poker!

Chapter Nine

Where Will it go From Here?

In this book I have covered and detailed every poker cheating method I know of. I cannot with unbiased confidence tell you that variations of cheating unknown to me do not exist. There are always people out there in the poker world feverishly dreaming up new ways to cheat you out of your money, and some of them are bound to come to fruition.

I can say, however, that the possibility of poker-cheating scams in existence that I cannot conceptualize is remote. My entire life has been lived in and around cheating at gambling. I have experimented with hundreds of methods geared up for cheating, some using equipment, others altering gaming equipment used by casinos and cardrooms. I have seen computerized cheating software aimed at online gambling and I have seen cheaters who use nothing more than their wits and balls, which often proves best.

Naturally after 30 years of immersion in this subject, I have formed opinions and theories concerning the ongoing evolution of poker cheating, the forces combatting it and the people on the frontlines of each side. The one thing I can tell you with the most conviction is that the poker-cheating war will go on as long as the game of poker itself. Again, wherever there is gambling, no matter what its shape or form, there will be those people looking to cheat at it, and those paid professionals trying to fight back the cheaters.

Of all the poker-cheating methods and scenarios I have described, collusion is far and away the best. It may not offer its instigators the fastest rate of return on their investments, but what makes it so preferable is that besides yielding a sure profit when executed effectively, it is the only structurally sound form of cheating I know of that can never really be proven, certainly not to the point where its perpetrators could be arrested and face prison time. This form of cheating will continue much in its present form through the ages.

In live poker games, nothing in the underworld needs to change. There is a limited number of coordinated techniques by which cheaters can signal one another the value of their hands. This will not be revolutionized. No one will come up with a variance of hand signalling better than using chip placements on cards. There are other clandestine procedures that get the job done as well, but no one will ever invent an "invisible" move with which Player A can tell Player B the value of his cards.

On the Internet, collusion is less likely to thrive indefinitely, but I still say it will be online for a long time to come. Here, too, collusion between online players is difficult to prove, although it is much easier for sites and players keeping track of played hands to prove that collusion is probably going on. That you can go back and trace an indefinite number of hands played online allows you to later analyze what had happened at your poker table after the session is over.

Your evaluation of the online game need not interfere with the game itself. But in live poker, once the cards are thrown in the muck there's no way to reconstruct the hand exactly as it had played out. And then you'd need to reconstruct several dozen hands to have even the smallest sample of what had taken place at your table. Gathering evidence of collusion in live poker is just not feasible.

Online, it will be up to the sites to decide whether they want to take stronger action on suspecting collusion teams in their games. I've mentioned before that a few sites have barred players they've alleged to have committed this infraction. Some have even frozen accounts, but these actions have been very infrequent in comparison to the number of investigations online sites claim their security personnel have conducted.

Perhaps one day the sites will come up with some kind of superintelligent "bot-cop" capable of identifying and stamping out colluders. However, I'd imagine that the federal government would find a legislative maneuver to stamp out online gambling in the US long before that ever happened, and I'm not sure it will ever happen.

On the big-time tournament circuit, the most significant change in the cheating syndicates will be an increase in their sheer sizes. Last year's WSOP championship event had 5,600 entries and 10% of them were paid prize money. The numbers of people participating not only at the WSOP but also in thousands of poker tournaments across the world are increasing by staggering figures. Just 10 years ago, the entries and number of events at the WSOP were a mere fraction of what they are now.

This upward trend will continue indefinitely. If current online poker revenues of $2.2 billion can be expected to increase to $9 billion by 2009, can we then expect to see 20,000 people participating in the championship event of the 2009 WSOP? Shit, they'd have to stage the thing in Las Vegas's Silver Bowl football stadium!

I'm not guaranteeing we'll see 20,000 people there, but we

will see more than we did in last year's record-breaking turn-out. As the number of participants increases each year so will the number of colluders. It's a symbiotic relationship. To maintain the same rates of return on their investments, professional cheating teams must increase their sizes to effectively offset the growing numbers of their non-colluding opponents.

For those of you getting ready to go to your local home game, nothing much will change on that front. If you've been lucky enough to have played all these years with your same trusted group, then you've got nothing to worry about and you can tell your poker-playing buddies how you've just finished this "really interesting poker-cheating book by Richard Marcus." If, on the other hand, you're in a game with a player or players whom you don't feel that trustworthy about, now you can pay specific attention to their habits and composure in your game and draw your own conclusion as to whether you want to tell them about my book.

I can tell you this, though. If your home game is like most normal home games, which over the years see a fair amount of infusions of new players and defections of old ones, you're most likely to run into some of those dangerous Ricky and Dicky characters we met before. At least now you'll be better prepared to handle them.

Finally, I feel confident that by reading this book you are now very well informed as to how extensive poker cheating is. And I know many of you have been concerned about it. Cheating at poker is starting to get some of the press that legitimate poker-playing has enjoyed for a few years now. I've read articles about it in *Maxim* magazine and others. Just recently I saw a show on Court TV called *Takedown*. Its premise is a band of casino-cheating artists that infiltrates casino security systems and "takes down" the casino for loads of money. The episode I saw teamed-up a professional card mechanic with the head of the cheating band in a Texas with the head of the cheating band in a Texas hold'em game designed to bust out five excellent poker players. The intended victims were actually in the dark about the cheating. They believed that the filming of their game was only for promotional purposes, or at least that is what the producers of the show have claimed.

The mechanic used on the show was very talented. He performed all the cheating techniques I have brought forth in this book. He culled cards, stacked the deck, fake shuffled, fake riffled, recovered the cut, peeked at the top card, dealt from the bottom, dealt the second card and even dealt the legitimate top card from time to time. Naturally the five players got busted out, and at the end told that they had been the victims of a poker scam.

I have seen some really bad TV shows about casino cheating, some of which are outright bullshit, but I must say that *Takedown*'s little display of a poker scam at work was very well pulled off. It showed how vulnerable honest players are when attacked by a dishonest dealer in cahoots with someone at the table.

In closing, I want to comment on some things out there I've been made aware of. People looking to rip you off have been spreading around the term "neocheating" as though it were some kind of gospel. This is supposed to be "cheating without cheating." Well, let me stop that buck right there. Cheating is cheating and not cheating is not cheating. It's as simple as that, black and white. These people are hawking neocheating so they can sell you underground books on how to go online and "cheat online poker games." They guarantee you an income of $25,000 per month. Then they quickly modify these bold statements to mean that the cheating you will actually do is not illegal although it might be against the policies of certain online poker sites.

Don't waste your money or your time with this stuff. The 25 grand they guarantee you plus a bus token will get you on the bus. The truth is that even the most skilled online professional cheaters using collusion tactics do not earn that kind of money, at least not consistently. The only way to cheat Internet poker to the tune of $300,000 a year is to use the cheating computer software and robots I have described, and those people with the cash and brainpower to do so would not invest a dime in any of these bogus books.

Finally, I imagine that after reading this book your general outlook on the poker world may have changed. There is nothing wrong with that. You are now just that much wiser. I'm sure that your newly acquired knowledge breeds certain questions concerning what sorts of action you should take regarding your poker future.

Should you continue playing in live cardrooms? Should you have faith in poker tournaments and not give up on your dream of one day winning that big one? Should you shun legitimate poker-playing completely and become a cheat?

NO! The answer to that last question is an unequivocal "no." The last thing I would want is for all you honest players out there, who make up the vast majority of the poker world, to become dishonest as I and other people have done. I've only taught you all these cheating methods so you can be better prepared to defend yourselves in the poker world. You should use this knowledge to evaluate the games and situations you find yourselves in while playing poker, both in live action and online. If you do that, I will have accomplished something by writing this book. I have shared my considerable knowledge with you and can only hope it has some positive effect on the future of poker across the world.

You should absolutely continue playing in live poker rooms. Just be a little more wary than you've been. Watch for the signs of collusion and other forms of cheating in live games that you're now familiar with. I can assure you that if you play often enough and maintain a steady degree of vigilance, you will pick up on some shady activities going on and you'll be able to choose your proper course of action.

You may also continue playing in your poker tournaments, but there you must constantly be on your toes. As tournaments move through their stages very quickly, the collusion groups take their swing the second the ball is pitched. They can easily accomplish a major ploy in the playing of a single hand. Remember that in tournament play a single key hand has much more of an impact than it would in a ring game. If you lose the wrong hand you're out of the tournament. In a ring game, all you'd need to do to recover is buy more chips.

One thing going for you honest players is that the publication of this book is sure to have a damaging effect on the cheaters. Knowing that you, their victims, have been wised up to their methods, they will have to tone down the frequency and extent of their moves. I'm not saying that my having exposed poker cheating as it really is will send all the cheating syndicates back to the drawing board, but I will say they will have much less of an advantage against you. I can also reassure you, especially in live-action poker, that even the Einsteins of poker cheating will not come up with anything new to enhance their ability to steal your money.

Online, neither I nor anyone else can accurately predict the future of Internet poker—or even if there is much of one. If assuming that online poker is here to stay for a while, we should make a parallel assumption that hackers and computer geniuses will continue designing programs to infiltrate online sites' software.

For now, the biggest threat to the online rooms, apart from the American government closing them down in the United

States, is that in the near future there will be no more human players left at the online table. Infallible high-tech bots may one day occupy each seat at every table online. If this happens in a perfect online world, we'll witness a future in which people using robots to play poker will go broke. That would happen in the assumption that one "superbot" is approximately as good as the next, and in the long run each would win the same number of different-sized pots.

Only the sites would come out ahead through their constant raking of pots, but they would eventually see all their players disappear. That's because, just like in the live poker world, players tire of consistently losing, and when they do they find somewhere else to play. In fact, I'll say that in ten years, online poker will have gone the way of dinosaurs.

Now that you're finally ready to put this book down and boot up your PC to your favorite online poker site, or jump in your car and drive it to the nearest poker club, or walk over to the high-stakes home-affair next-door, let me wish you the best of luck in your game.

But please, don't cheat or be cheated.

And drop me a line to tell me about those big pots you're winning!

Final word

In 2005, my ex-partner Preacher won a major WSOP event. I was very happy for him. Another professional player who briefly worked with me in the casinos won a major WPT event. They each worked in collusion for their titles. They told me so.

Praise for Richard Marcus' previous book titled *American Roulette* in the US and *Great Casino Heist* in Europe.

"*American Roulette* provides the titillating thrill of being welcomed inside a forbidden world… Marcus and his gang of thieves have a brazen ingenuity, and enterprising criminal spirit that's hard to resist. *American Roulette* is as fun as it is revealing."

Michael Konik, author of *Telling Lies and Getting Paid* and *The Man with the $100,000 Breasts and other Gambling Stories*.

"Richard Marcus is that rarest of tour guides: a real insider who offers an unvarnished account of how he cheated casinos out of tidy little piles of money...a rare tell-all."

Timothy L. O'Brien, author of *Bad Bet: The Inside Story of the Glamour, Glitz, and Danger of America's Gambling Industry*.

"So much fun to read that this book deserves to be in two sections of every bookstore – Crime and Magic. One of the most original books on gambling and Las Vegas that I've ever read."

Bert Randolph Sugar, author of *The Caesar's Palace Sports Book of Betting*.

"It's a shame that Hollywood's Rat Pack is no more, because Marcus's account of his career cheating casinos (he is now retired-and not in a jail cell) would be the perfect vehicle for Old Blue Eyes, Dino, and the gang. It features high rollers, exotic locales, beautiful women, a detective obsessed with busting the protagonist, and tension in every move."

Library Journal.

"*American Roulette* qualifies as a great book...a fascinating study in the hows and wherefores of casino cheating, as well as casino security...while Marcus is hardly a role model, his account is an interesting and often suspenseful glimpse into a world of which relatively few are aware. Recommended."

Bookreporter.com

"Marcus (never caught and now retired) is likable and creates suspense as he takes on casino after casino...Readers find vicarious thrills sharing the rush of risking thousands of dollars against years in a Nevada prison."

Publishers Weekly

"In this memoir, a grafter with a predator's understanding of human frailty recounts his true adventures swindling casinos the world over. Marcus's prose is so detail-rich it's as if you're fattening your pockets and running from the "steam" (ie angry casino muscle) right alongside him."

Details Magazine

"*American Roulette: Confessions Of A Cheat* makes for fascinating reading. How Marcus and his team circumvented security measures and got away with their cheating make for some fascinating reading. This is a fascinating, well-detailed book. It should be read by anyone who thinks its easy to cheat, but might not realize how dangerous it is and the consequence if caught. Marcus survived, retired and has no regrets about his lifestyle. Few have been so lucky."

CasinoCityTimes.com

"American Roulette is a fascinating story not only for those who occasionally casino-gamble, but for everyone with a little larceny in their heart."

High Stakes Bookshop

"While the dish that casinos serve may be illusory and never satisfying, American Roulette treats us to a feast where, for once, the tables have been turned."

Las Vegas Mercury

"A great book...Marcus reveals entirely believable tales of how he swapped out chips and pulled all sorts of other scams against the Evil Empire."

Detroit Free Press

"*American Roulette* informs the non-cheater of an interesting world of manipulative psychology that goes into conning dealers and planning heists."

Las Vegas Weekly

"One of the most successful the game has ever seen... Reveals how he scammed over one million dollars without getting caught."

Entertainment Tonight